The Law for Institutes of Consecrated Life and Societies of Apostolic Life

An Introduction to Canons 573–746

Daniel Tibi, OSB

LITURGICAL PRESS
Collegeville, Minnesota

litpress.org

Cover design by Monica Bokinskie

Library of Congress Cataloging-in-Publication Data

Names: Tibi, Daniel, author.
Title: The law for institutes of consecrated life and societies of apostolic life : an introduction to Canons 573-746 / Daniel Tibi, OSB.
Description: Collegeville, Minnesota : Liturgical Press, 2025. | Includes bibliographical references. | Summary: "This book provides an up-to-date, comprehensive presentation of the Law of Institutes of Consecrated Life and Societies of Apostolic Life according to the 1983 Code of Canon Law. It is intended as an introduction for superiors and members of institutes and societies, as well as for vicars and officials in ecclesiastical administration. It will also serve as a useful resource for novitiate formation, and an initial overview for students engaged in academic study"—Provided by publisher.
Identifiers: LCCN 2025013220 (print) | LCCN 2025013221 (ebook) | ISBN 9798400802003 (trade paperback) | ISBN 9798400802010 (epub) | ISBN 9798400802294 (pdf)
Subjects: LCSH: Monasticism and religious orders (Canon law) | Catholic Church. Codex Juris Canonici (1983) | BISAC: RELIGION / Christian Church / Canon & Ecclesiastical Law | RELIGION / Monasticism
Classification: LCC KBU2899 .T53 2025 (print) | LCC KBU2899 (ebook) | DDC 262.9/42—dc23/eng/20250326
LC record available at https://lccn.loc.gov/2025013220
LC ebook record available at https://lccn.loc.gov/2025013221

"Daniel Tibi has written a concise, up-to-date, and easy-to-read commentary on the canons applicable to religious life. He understands the differences between the various expressions of religious life and how the canons apply within the context of the various expressions. Leadership will find very helpful the excellent summaries and listings of materials required for seeking approvals and indults from the Dicastery for Institutes of Consecrated Life and Societies of Apostolic Life."

— Dan Ward, OSB

"Daniel Tibi provides a thorough discussion and review of the canons which apply to institutes of consecrated life. Of particular value may be the sections with background and application of the norms to be observed when difficulties arise around a member's status or when hierarchical recourse is needed. The text is a good complement to the different handbooks, especially by the professional societies of canon law, that exist. Tibi's work serves as a good refresher as well as a source for changes in the canons on consecrated life that have occurred since the 1983 Code was promulgated."

— Lynn Jarrell, OSU

"Canon lawyer Daniel Tibi, OSB, offers an accessible commentary to the canonical norms on consecrated life in the Roman Catholic Church. It includes all changes in the law that have come about over the past forty years. A valuable commentary for those living in consecrated life as well as to those in leadership and their advisors, be it within a religious institute or a diocese."

— Myriam Wijlens, professor of canon law,
University of Erfurt, and member of the
Pontifical Commission for the Protection
of Minors (2018–2022)

Contents

Part II

Societies of Apostolic Life

Foreword

Since the current Code of Canon Law came into force in 1983, its wording has been amended thirteen times, eleven of which were made during Pope Francis's pontificate. Five of these amendments concern the law for institutes of consecrated life and societies of apostolic life. In addition, there have been two changes in church law promulgated outside the context of the Code that have not affected it wording. One notable trend in these legal changes is decentralization and the strengthening of subsidiarity. Institutes of consecrated life and societies of apostolic life have been given more faculties to handle their own affairs. However, more competence also means more responsibility and requires a precise knowledge of the law.

This book offers an up-to-date overall presentation of the law for institutes of consecrated life and societies of apostolic life according to the 1983 Code of Canon Law. It is aimed at superiors, formation directors, and members of institutes and societies, as well as diocesan administrators, to provide them with an introduction to this area of canon law. In the academic field, it offers an initial overview to students.

The structure of this book is based on that of the third part of the second book of the Code of Canon Law on "Institutes of Consecrated Life and Societies of Apostolic Life" (cc. 573–746). In this way, it is easier to read this book in parallel with the norms of the Code. Individual sections of this book are accompanied by suggestions for further reading, which can offer a more in-depth examination of a topic.

Introduction

Religious life has charismatic origins, and the spiritual element was essential from the start. There were no written rules or fixed organizational structures. The early Christian hermits were guided in their monastic life by the word of God in the Bible and the counsel of experienced monks who served as spiritual fathers. After its charismatic origins, monastic life was first organized and structured by Pachomius, who, in the fourth century, was the first to write a monastic rule for cenobitic monks.[1] Thus, the juridical element came into religious life alongside the spiritual element. A monastic life lived solely on one's own responsibility requires a strong self-discipline not to neglect the monastic observance. The regulations of the monastic rule protect the monastic observance and provide an organizational framework in which it may be lived. The author of the Rule of St. Benedict, a sixth-century monastic rule, calls his Rule "*lex*"—law (RB 58.10, 15). It organizes monastic life, but the Rule is also a spiritual guide for monastic life according to the will of God (see RB Prol 45; 73.1, 8-9). This view of the law as a guide for living according to the will of God has a biblical basis. After the exodus, the law given by God to the Israelites was seen as God's gift to his people, distinguishing Israel from all other nations, revealing the way of justice, and ensuring peace (see Deut 4:1-8). It is no coincidence that law entered monastic life when a cenobitic form of

[1] For further details, see David Knowles, *From Pachomius to Ignatius: A Study in the Constitutional History of the Religious Orders* (Clarendon, 1966).

monastic life was established. For hermits living alone in the desert, some oral rules might have been sufficient, but at least since hermits formed loose associations, as in the Desert of Scetis, some basic rules for living together were necessary. For cenobitic monks, a rule organizing their life together was and is necessary. Thus, the place of law in religious life is to build community by establishing the organizational structures and by clarifying the mutual rights and obligations. In religious life, law is not an end in itself but remains a means to an end. Therefore, "canonical equity is to be observed, and the salvation of souls, which must always be the supreme law in the Church, is to be kept before one's eyes" (c. 1752).[2]

That law is a means to an end implies that law must not be rigid but an aid to achieving the end of religious life. The constant renewal of the law, especially the law for religious communities, was an important concern of the Second Vatican Council. The principal document of the Second Vatican Council on religious life is the decree *Perfectae Caritatis* (October 28, 1965), on the adaptation and renewal of religious life. This decree deals primarily with the theological foundations of religious life, but it also made it necessary that "constitutions, directories, books of customs, of prayers, of ceremonies and such like should be suitably revised, obsolete prescriptions being suppressed, and should be brought into line with this synod's documents."[3]

[2] All English quotations from the Code in this volume are taken from *Code of Canon Law: Latin-English Edition*, 4th printing (Canon Law Society of America, 2023).

[3] Second Vatican Council, Decree on the Up-to-date Renewal of Religious Life *Perfectae Caritatis*, October 28, 1965 (hereafter, PC), no. 3. All quotations of Vatican II documents are from Austin Flannery, ed., *Vatican Council II: Constitutions, Decrees, Declarations: A Completely Revised Translation in Inclusive Language* (Liturgical Press, 2014).

Pope Paul VI's apostolic letter *Ecclesiae Sanctae* (August 6, 1966)[4] contains provisions for implementing this mandate. Within two or three years, each institute was to convene an ordinary or extraordinary general chapter to carry out the renewal of religious life initiated by the council (ES II,3). The task of implementing the renewal of religious life was entrusted to the institutes themselves, and the general chapters were called not only to make laws but especially to promote spiritual and apostolic vitality (ES II,1). Matters that were obsolete, subject to change according to a particular era, or that merely reflected local customs were to be excluded from the constitutions (ES II,14). To be considered obsolete were those things which did not constitute the nature and purpose of the institute, which had lost their meaning and power, and which were no longer of real help to religious life (ES II,17). Renewal was to be carried out in collaboration between superiors and all members (ES II,2). A full and free consultation of the members was to take place, and the results were to be organized in such a way as to help the work of the general chapters (ES II,4). The general chapters of renewal, which could be divided into two distinct periods separated by no more than one year (ES II,3), had the right to change the constitutions *ad experimentum*, as long as the purpose, nature, and character of the institute were preserved. Even changes contrary to universal law were not excluded, if they seemed reasonable and were authorized by the Apostolic See (ES II,6). The modification *ad experimentum* was to remain in force until the next ordinary general chapter, which could decide to continue them until the next chapter (ES II,6). The final approval of the constitutions after the probationary period was reserved to the competent authority (ES II,8). The Jesuit

[4] Hereafter, ES. Available at https://www.vatican.va/content/paul-vi/en/motu_proprio/documents/hf_p-vi_motu-proprio_19660806_ecclesiae-sanctae.html.

Jean Beyer, a contemporary witness to the renewal process, called this endeavor "at once grace-giving and breath-taking."[5] In a relatively short period of time, institutes had to define their own identity, faithful to the will of their founders, and adapt their life to the needs of the present time.

The revised Code of Canon Law was promulgated by John Paul II on January 25, 1983, and came into force on the first Sunday of Advent of the same year, November 27, 1983, which made it necessary to further revise the proper law of institutes of consecrated life and societies of apostolic life, to adapt it to the new universal law.

Since the 1983 Code of Canon Law came into force, thirteen amendments have been made, five of which concern the law of institutes of consecrated life and societies of apostolic life. Those five were all made by Pope Francis. They, and the apostolic letters through which they were made, are:

- cc. 694 and 729: *Communis Vita* (March 19, 2019)
- c. 579: *Authenticum Charismatis* (November 1, 2020)
- cc. 604 §3, 686 §§1–2, 699 §2, and 700: *Competentias Quasdam* (February 11, 2022)
- c. 695 §1: *Recognitum Librum VI* (April 26, 2022)
- c. 700: *Expedit ut Iura* (April 2, 2023)

In addition, two changes of the law have not altered the wording of the Code of Canon Law. They are:

- Congregation for Institutes of Consecrated Life and Societies of Apostolic Life, Instruction on the Implementation of the Apostolic Constitution *Vultum Dei Quaerere* on Women's Contemplative Life *Cor Orans* (April 1, 2018),

[5] Jean Beyer, "Prospects for the Reform of Religious Constitutions," *The Way Supplement* 26 (1975): 88.

introducing several changes of the law approved by Pope Francis *in forma specifica* concerning nuns[6]

- Francis, Rescript of the Holy Father Francis Regarding the Derogation from Can. 588 §2 *Rescriptum ex Audientia Sanctissimi* (May 18, 2022), granting the Dicastery for Institutes of Consecrated Life and Societies of Apostolic Life the faculty to derogate from c. 588 §2 in individual cases and allow lay members of clerical institutes to assume the office of superior[7]

[6] According to the 1917 Code of Canon Law, nuns were "women religious with solemn vows" (c. 488 7° CIC/1917). The 1983 Code of Canon Law does not define the term. According to the instruction *Cor Orans*, the term "in addition to the religious of solemn vows, refers to those who profess simple vows in monasteries, both perpetual as temporary. The Church, among the women consecrated to God through the profession of the evangelical counsels, designates only to nuns the commitment of public prayer, raising to God in its name the Divine Office as a praying community to be celebrated in chorus. The legitimate name nun is not opposed to: 1) the simple profession emitted legitimately in monasteries; 2) the exercise of apostolic works joined to contemplative life whether by approved institution and confirmed by the Holy See for some orders, or for legitimate prescription or concession by the Holy See in favor of some monasteries" (CO 1–2). For further details, see Nancy Bauer, "*Moniales et sorores*: The Canonical Distinction Between Nuns and Sisters with Particular Reference to Benedictine Women Religious," *ABR* 70 (2019): 45–73.

[7] The text of the rescript was originally published in Italian, at press. https://press.vatican.va/content/salastampa/it/bollettino/pubblico/2022/05/18/0371/00782.html. There is no official English translation. An unofficial English translation is available at ofmconv.net/en/i-fratelli-laici-possono-diventare-superiori-maggiori.

Abbreviations

AAS	*Acta Apostolicae Sedis*
ABR	*The American Benedictine Review*
CCCB	Canadian Conference of Catholic Bishops
CCEO	*Codex Canonum Ecclesiarum Orientalium* (Code of Canons of the Eastern Churches)
CD	*Christus Dominus*
CIC	*Codex Iuris Canonici* (Code of Canon Law)
CICLSAL	Congregation for Institutes of Consecrated Life and Societies of Apostolic Life
CLD	*Canon Law Digest*
CLSA	Canon Law Society of America
CLSA Proceedings	*Proceedings of the Annual Convention of the Canon Law Society of America*
CO	*Cor Orans*
Comm	*Communicationes*
CpRM	*Commentarium pro Religiosis et Missionariis*
DICLSAL	Dicastery for Institutes of Consecrated Life and Societies of Apostolic Life
ES	*Ecclesiae Sanctae*
ESI	*Ecclesiae Sponsae Imago*
GoF	*The Gift of Fidelity, The Joy of Perserverence*

IC	*Ius Canonicum*
Jur	*The Jurist*
KiP	*Kościół i Prawo*
LPSA	*Lex propria Signaturae Apostolicae*
ME	*Monitor Ecclesiasticus*
MR	*Mutuae Relationes*
PC	*Perfectae Caritatis*
PE	*Praedicate Evangelium*
PRC	*Periodica de Re Canonica*
QDE	*Quaderni di Diritto Ecclesiale*
RB	*Regula Benedicti* (Rule of St. Benedict)
RfR	*Review for Religious*
RRAO	*Roman Replies and CLSA Advisory Opinions*
StudCan	*Studia Canonica*
USCCB	United States Conference of Catholic Bishops
VC	*Vita Consecrata*

Part I

Institutes of Consecrated Life

Chapter One

Norms Common to All Institutes of Consecrated Life (cc. 573–606)

The 1983 Code of Canon Law deals with institutes of consecrated life and societies of apostolic life in the third part of the second book, in cc. 573–606. The Code does not use an umbrella term for institutes of consecrated life and societies of apostolic life.[1] Institutes of consecrated life are divided into religious institutes and secular institutes. Religious institutes can be divided into orders and congregations, although the 1983 Code no longer makes this distinction.[2] Orders can be further subdivided into monastic orders (e.g., Benedictines, Cistercians, Trappists, Carthusians), canons regular (e.g., Canons Regular of St. Augustine, Premonstratensians), military and hospitaller orders (e.g., Sovereign Military Order of Malta, Teutonic Order), mendicant orders (e.g., Order of Preachers, Order of Friars Minor), and clerics regular (e.g., Theatines, Society of Jesus, Camillians).

[1] The Munich school of canon law coined the term "associations of canonical life" (*kanonische Lebensverbände*) as an umbrella term.

[2] According to the 1917 Code of Canon Law, orders were religious institutes in which solemn vows were taken, and congregations were religious institutes in which only simple vows were taken (see c. 488 no. 2 CIC/1917). Although the 1983 Code no longer makes this distinction, it can still be found in the proper law of some institutes.

The norms regarding institutes of consecrated life are to be found in the second part of the second book of the Code. Norms common to all institutes of consecrated life are listed in cc. 573–606, followed by the norms specifically concerning religious institutes in cc. 607–709 and the norms specifically concerning secular institutes cc. 710–730.

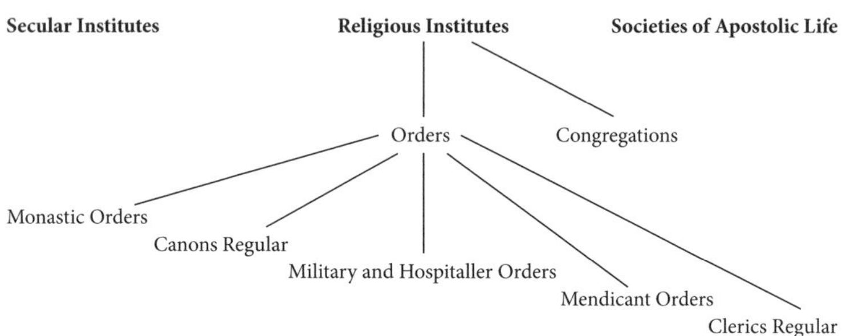

Typology of Institutes of Consecrated Life and Societies of Apostolic Life

1. Fundamentals of Consecrated Life (cc. 573–577)

Consecrated life[3] cannot be treated in mere legal categories. Its theological foundation, too, must be taken into consideration. Canons 573–577 contain fundamental theological statements. The source of this theological foundation of consecrated life is the relevant statements of the Second Vatican Council. In addition to fundamental theological statements, these canons also have legal content.

Consecrated life is characterized by two aspects: It is a stable form of living that is established through the profession of the evangelical counsels (see c. 573 §1). This definition ap-

[3] The term "consecrated life" (*vita consacrata*) first came into use at the time of the Second Vatican Council, before which, in reference to Matthew 19:21, the common expression was "state of perfection" (*status perfectionis*), which was abandoned in order to avoid the misunderstanding of superiority to other Christian states of life.

plies to both religious institutes and secular institutes. The special characteristic of religious institutes is that the members "lead a life of brothers or sisters in common" (c. 607 §2), and the special characteristic of secular institutes is that the members are "Christian faithful, living in the world" (c. 710). Consecrated life is intended to be permanent. This is not contradicted by the fact that profession is initially made temporarily. Those who are admitted to temporary profession should have the general intention of remaining in the institute permanently, even if they may later decide against a lifelong commitment. To enter consecrated life only for a certain period of time is not legally possible. Profession has both a spiritual and a legal dimension. Firstly and foremost, profession is a religious act. As an act of worship, it is a self-surrender to God. Secondly, profession is also a legal act through which the professed receives a new status within the church. The profession incorporates the professed into a specific institute. Therefore, profession has a contractual character and binds both the professed and the institute. In particular, the professed person submits themself to the full availability of the institute within the framework of the norms of universal law and the proper law of the institute. The institute assumes an obligation to provide for the professed person. Profession includes a commitment to the evangelical counsels of chastity, poverty, and obedience (see c. 573 §2). It is up to the competent ecclesiastical authority to interpret the evangelical counsels and to direct their practice (see c. 576). The concrete way in which the evangelical counsels are lived in the individual institutes can vary. There are institutes that add an institute-specific fourth vow to the three vows of the evangelical counsels.[4] Members of

[4] See Johannes Günter Gerhartz, *"Insuper promitto . . .": Die feierlichen Sondergelübde katholischer Orden*, Series Facultatis Iuris Canonici / B 19 (Editrice Pontificia Università Gregoriana, 1966). Members of the Society of Jesus, for instance, take the following fourth vow: "I further promise a special obedience to the sovereign pontiff in regard to the missions, accord-

Benedictine institutes commit themselves in their profession to obedience, stability, and conversion to the monastic way of life, which includes the commitment to the evangelical counsels. The essential principles of the evangelical counsels that apply to all institutes are mentioned in cc. 599–601. Institutes of consecrated life have different forms and traditions. What they all have in common is the following of Christ, which emphasizes one aspect depending on the charism of an institute (see c. 577). Contemplative institutes more closely follow Christ who prays. Institutes with active apostolic work follow Christ who announces the kingdom of God or does good to people. Secular institutes follow Christ who lives with people in the world yet who always does the will of the Father. This very schematic categorization has recently devolved into a fluid transition of different charisms within the same institute.

2. Patrimony (c. 578)

The patrimony is the spiritual heritage of an institute. It consists of two poles, namely, the mind and designs of the founder regarding the nature, purpose, spirit, and character of an institute, which have been sanctioned by competent ecclesiastical authority, on the one hand and the sound tradition[5] on the other (see c. 578).

The source of this canon in the documents of the Second Vatican Council is *Perfectae Caritatis* 2(b): "It is to the church's advantage that each institute has its own proper character and function. Therefore the spirit and aims of each founder should

---

ing to the same apostolic letters [of the Society of Jesus] and the constitutions" (*Constitutiones Societatis Iesu*, 527). See John W. O'Malley, "The Fourth Vow in Its Ignatian Context: A Historical Study," *Studies in the Spirituality of Jesuits* 15 (1983): 1–59.

[5] The concept of "sound tradition" (*sana traditio*) means that not everything that has been introduced in the course of the history of the institute is part of its patrimony, but only what has contributed to its development.

be faithfully acknowledged and maintained, as indeed should each institute's sound traditions, for all of these constitute an institute's heritage."

Every institute was initiated under the influence of the Holy Spirit by a particular person in a concrete time and under concrete circumstances. It has been approved by the competent authority of the church. It is under the influence of the same Spirit that future generations are attracted to the way of life of the founder and adopt it as their own. They live the patrimony of their institute in their own concrete time and under their own concrete circumstances. This way, the patrimony is renewed from generation to generation. The patrimony is dynamic, not static. Every generation has, in a way, to re-found its institute faithful to the mind and designs of the founder and to ask itself how the charism of the founder can be authentically lived in its own time. The founder of an institute was attentive to the signs of her or his time and reacted to them according to the charism she or he had received from the Holy Spirit. Future generations of the institute should be attentive to the signs of their own time to keep the spirit of the institute alive under the new and changed circumstances of their time. This includes returning to the original spirit of the institute and adapting it to the circumstances of the present time. In this way, the patrimony of an institute is in constant development. Institutes easily run the risk of making the founder's will absolute and disregarding tradition in its historical development. However, both elements must be given due consideration. The patrimony of an institute is the patrimony as it is lived in the present.

This patrimony is to be faithfully preserved by all, which includes members and superiors of the institute as well as the ecclesiastical authority, especially bishops. The members of the institute are called to orient their lives to the patrimony of their institute. The general chapter of a religious institute is obliged "to protect the patrimony of the institute mentioned in can. 578" and to "promote suitable renewal according to that patrimony" (c. 631 §1). The ecclesiastical authority is responsible "to take care that the institutes grow and flourish according to the spirit of the founders and sound traditions" (c. 576). For this reason, the Code grants due autonomy to the institutes so that they can "preserve their own patrimony intact, as mentioned in can. 578" (c. 586 §1). This includes a statutory autonomy of the institutes, whose fundamental legal norms must be rooted in its patrimony (see c. 587 §1).

Further reading: Fabio Ciardi, "Il carisma del fondatore," *Annales theologici* 30 (2016): 141–58; Nicolas de Boccard, *Charisme et instituts de vie consacré: Les canons 578 et 587 du code de droit canonique de 1983*, Romanité et modernité du droit 22 (DeBoccard, 2015); John C. Futrell, "Discovering the Founder's Charism," *The Way* 14 (1971): 62–70; Giancarlo Rocca, "Il Carisma del Fondatore," *Claretianum* 34 (1994): 31–105; Yuji Sugawara, "Concetto teologico e giuridico del 'carisma di fondazione' degli istituti di vita consacrata," *PRC* 91 (2002): 239–71.

3. Erection of Institutes of Consecrated Life (c. 579)

The erection of a new institute is usually preceded by the foundation of an association of the faithful (see cc. 298–329). Although the establishment of a new institute is legally possible directly by the Apostolic See (see c. 589), the normal case is that a new institute is established at the diocesan level. The ecclesiastical authority is concerned that new institutes are not founded without the necessary cautions. Whether an institute brings with it a new charism and whether it is capable of development and stability must be carefully examined. The Fourth Lateran Council (1215) determined that new foundations of religious orders fall within the competence of the Apostolic See and forbade the introduction of new rules. In

Perfectae Caritatis 19, the Second Vatican Council states, regarding the foundation of new institutes: "When it is proposed to found a new religious institute it must be asked, seriously: is it necessary, or at least very useful, and can it develop? Otherwise, institutes may be imprudently founded which are useless or lacking in sufficient vitality."

The 1978 document of the Sacred Congregation for Religious and Secular Institutes and the Sacred Congregation for Bishops, *Mutuae Relationes*, goes into further detail and specifies:

> In some regions there is noticeable a certain overabundance of initiatives to found new religious institutes. Those who are responsible for discerning the authenticity of each foundation should weigh with humility, of course, but also objectively, constantly, and seeking to foresee clearly the future possibilities. . . . In fact, when judgment regarding the establishment of an institute is formulated only in view of its usefulness and suitability in the field of action, or simply on the basis of the comportment of some person who experiences devotional phenomena, in themselves ambiguous, then indeed it becomes evident that the genuine concept of religious life in the Church is in a certain manner distorted.
>
> To pronounce judgment on the authenticity of a charism, the following characteristics are required:
>
> a) its special origin from the Spirit, distinct, even though not separate, from special personal talents, which become apparent in the sphere of activity and organization;
>
> b) a profound ardor of love to be conformed to Christ in order to give witness to some aspect of His mystery;
>
> c) a constructive love of the Church, which absolutely shrinks from causing any discord in Her.
>
> . . . When there is question, therefore, of new foundations, all who have a role to play in passing judgment must

> express their opinions with great prudence, patient appraisal and just demands. (MR 51)

The 1983 Code of Canon Law grants the authority to establish a new institute to the competent diocesan bishop (see c. 579). However, this authority has been reduced over time. Initially, c. 579 provided that the diocesan bishop could establish a new institute by formal decree after consultation with the Apostolic See. If the diocesan bishop failed to consult the Apostolic See, a decree of erection was illicit but nevertheless valid. In 2007, the Congregation for Institutes of Consecrated Life and Societies of Apostolic Life compiled a list of the documents that must be submitted when the diocesan bishop consults the Apostolic See:

1. Historical and legal report on the association from its beginnings. The report must contain the following points in particular:
    a) name of the founder; purpose of the foundation; date and place of the beginning; name of the diocesan bishop who authorized the new foundation
    b) number and names of the first members
    c) construction, date, and location of the first novitiate house; name of the bishop who authorized to build the novitiate house; number of first novices and the date of their admission to the novitiate; number of candidates and the date of their first profession; name of the director of novices; names of those other than the director of novices who were responsible for the initial formation of the first members
    d) dates of the general chapters held
    e) name of the diocesan bishop who approved the first constitutions
    f) apostolic activity of the association at the beginning and in the present

   g) expansion of the association to other dioceses
   h) spirituality of the association

Indication where those preparing to receive ordination are trained.

2. Curriculum vitae of the founder of the association: name; date and place of birth and baptism; names of parents; education; other important events in his life

3. Curriculum vitae of the first superior general of the association. In addition to the above-mentioned information: date of entry into the association and of temporary and perpetual profession; date of appointment or election as superior general; modalities of appointment or election and term of office; current circumstances of life

4. Statistics of members and houses: names of temporary and perpetual professed, priests, novices and postulants; age of professed and priests; number of candidates and date of the next temporary and perpetual profession; number of houses in which the members live; names of the dioceses in which the association is present. The erection of an institute of diocesan right requires at least forty professed members, the majority of whom must have taken perpetual vows.

5. Financial report: amount of debt; amount of funds deposited with banks (if possible in US$ or euros); number of properties owned by the association.

6. Statements on the following points:
   a) whether there have been any unusual events, such as visions or similar
   b) whether there is another institute with the same name or the same charism in the diocese of the principal seat

7. Description of the habit

8. Three copies of the current constitutions and, if there is one, of the directory
9. Letters of recommendation from all the diocesan bishops concerned, including the bishop of the principal seat, to be sent directly to the dicastery and containing statements on the following points:
   a) usefulness and stability of the association
   b) discipline of the members
   c) liturgy and administration of the sacraments
   d) attitude towards the church and collaboration with the ecclesiastical authority
   e) initial and further formation
   f) financial management
   g) ability to take responsibility for the management of an institute that is present in various dioceses

If possible, a deposit of €500 to be paid to the cash office of the Dicastery for Institutes of Consecrated Life and Societies of Apostolic Life, which will be cleared at the end of the procedure.[6]

In a rescript dated May 11, 2016, Pope Francis stated that "prior consultation with the Apostolic See is to be understood as necessary *ad validitatem* before establishing of a diocesan Institute of consecrated life, otherwise risking nullity of the decree of establishment of this said Institute."[7] This new regulation came into force on June 1, 2016. In the administrative practice of the Apostolic See, a decree is issued at the end of the consultation, permitting or prohibiting the erection; such

[6] See Alberto Perlasca, "Rescriptum ex audientia SS.mi circa l'erezione degli istituti diocesani di vita consacrata (can. 579)," *QDE* 30 (2017): 356–57.

[7] Pope Francis, "Rescript ex Audientia Concerning Canon 579 of the Code of Canon Law on the Erection of a Diocesan Institute (11 May 2016)," *RRAO* 2016: 10–11.

a decree of permission is now required for the validity of the erection of an institute. This practice was de facto tantamount to a right of approval by the Apostolic See. In the apostolic letter *Authenticum Charismatis* of November 1, 2020, Pope Francis emphasizes the importance and necessity of a careful examination before erecting a new institute in order "to prevent the proliferation of institutions similar to one another, with the consequent risk of a harmful fragmentation into excessively small groups."[8] As institutes of consecrated life play an important role in the church, their erection goes beyond the diocesan level only. Effective November 10, 2020, Pope Francis amended c. 579, so that the diocesan bishop needs the written approval of the Apostolic See to validly erect an institute of consecrated life in his territory by formal decree. If the diocesan bishop fails to obtain the written approval from the Apostolic See, a decree of erection is invalid. With its legally valid erection, the institute acquires personality as a public juridic person by the law itself (see c. 116 §2).

Further reading: Rodger Austin, "Commentary: *Motu Proprio* of Pope Francis *Authenticum Charismatis*," *The Canonist* 11 (2020): 189–96; Pope Francis, "Rescript ex Audientia Concerning Canon 579 of the Code of Canon Law on the Erection of a Diocesan Institute (11 May 2016)," *RRAO* 2016: 10–11; Pope Francis, "Apostolic Letter *Authenticum charismatis* (1 November 2020)," *RRAO* 2021: 59–60; Amy Hereford, *See I Am Making Something New: A Canonical and Pastoral Guidebook on New Institutes, Diocesan Hermits and Consecrated Virgins and New Forms of Consecrated Life* (CreateSpace, 2018); Eileen C. Jaramillo, "Erection as an Institute of Consecrated Life or a Society of Apostolic Life: The Nuts and Bolts," *CLSA Proceedings* 80 (2018): 153–73.

[8] Pope Francis, "Apostolic Letter *Authenticum charismatis* (1 November 2020)," *RRAO* 2021: 59–60.

4. Aggregation (c. 580)

Aggregation (*aggregatio*) is the establishment of a spiritual community between two institutes, especially for apostolic purposes or to aggregate a third order. Both institutes retain their full canonical autonomy. The superior of the aggregating institute does not become the superior of the aggregated institute. The aggregation of an institute to another is reserved to the competent authority of the aggregating institute according to its proper law.

5. Mergers and Unions, Confederations and Federations (c. 582)

Mergers and unions, as well as confederations and federations, are reserved to the Apostolic See (see c. 582).

a) Merger

A merger (*fusio*) is the complete absorption of one institute into another. That is, one institute retains its previous legal personality and the other institute loses its previous legal personality and is completely absorbed into the institution with which it is merged.

b) Association

Association (*unio*) means that two or more institutes form a new institute. That is, all institutes lose their previous legal personality and a new juridic person emerges.

c) Federation

A federation is the union of several autonomous institutes under one superior. In practice, federations usually take the form of a monastic or canonical congregation or a federation of autonomous monasteries of nuns.

A monastic or canonical congregation is an association of several autonomous houses under one superior (e.g., abbot president, archabbot, or abbot general). The superior of a monastic or canonical congregation is a major superior (see c. 620) and the supreme moderator (see c. 622).

According to *Cor Orans*, a federation of autonomous monasteries of nuns is "a structure of communion among monasteries of the same Institute erected by the Apostolic See so that monasteries which share the same charism do not remain isolated but keep it faithfully and, giving each other mutual fraternal help, live the indispensable value of communion" (CO 86). It "is made up of several autonomous monasteries that have affinity of spirit and traditions and even if they are not necessarily configured according to a geographical criterion, as far as possible, they must not be geographically too distant" (CO 87). The monasteries of nuns that are members of the federation retain their autonomy and continue to be entrusted to the special vigilance of the diocesan bishop (see c. 615). The president of the federation is neither a major superior nor the supreme moderator. The scope of her authority is laid down in *Cor Orans* 110–22. In addition, *Cor Orans* grants her further powers that previously lay in the hands of the diocesan bishop, which strengthens the autonomy of the monasteries.

Federations are public juridic persons under canon law (see c. 116 §2), with the peculiarity that they are not an association of physical persons but of juridic persons.

d) Confederation

A confederation is the union of several federations under one superior. In practice, they occur in particular in the form of confederations of monastic or canonical congregations (e.g., the Benedictine Confederation, the Cistercian Order, or the Confederation of the Canons Regular of St. Augustine) under a common superior (e.g., abbot primate or abbot general). The superior of a confederation of monastic or canonical congregations is a major superior who does not, however, have all the power which universal law grants to major superiors (see c. 620). The scope of his authority is regulated in the proper law of the confederation. Different federations of autonomous monasteries of nuns of the same institute can, with the approval of the Apostolic See, constitute a confederation (see CO 95). Confederations are public juridic persons under canon law (see c. 116 §2), with the peculiarity that they are not an association of physical but juridic persons.

6. Changes in Institutes of Consecrated Life (c. 583)

What has been approved by the Apostolic See cannot be changed without its permission (see c. 583). Such matters are thus removed from the competence of the internal authority of the institute or from the competence the diocesan bishop.

7. Suppression (c. 584)

An institute of consecrated life as a public juridic person is perpetual by its nature (see c. 120 §1). Canon 584 mentions only one way an institute as a public juridic person can be extinguished, namely, by legitimate suppression by the competent authority. The suppression of an institute of consecrated life, both of diocesan right and pontifical right, pertains only to the Apostolic See (see c. 584). Thus, a diocesan bishop can erect an institute with the written approval of the Apostolic See but cannot suppress an institute once it has been legitimately founded. Therefore, c. 584 is an exception to the general principle that the authority that creates can also extinguish. The suppression of the only house of a religious institute usually means de facto the suppression of the institute, so this also pertains only to the Apostolic See (see c. 616 §2).[9] The other way an institute as a public juridic person can be extinguished is not explicitly mentioned in c. 584 but results from the general norms regarding public juridic persons in c. 120 §1: An institute of consecrated life is extinguished by the law itself if it has ceased to act for a hundred years. However, an institute of consecrated life does not have the right to dissolve itself by a decision of its members.

The decision regarding the temporal goods of a suppressed institute is also reserved to the Apostolic See (see cc. 584; 616 §2). The temporal goods do not necessarily become the property of the Apostolic See, which is only entitled to decide how the temporal goods are to be used. A provision in this regard in the proper law of the institute is not binding for the Apostolic See; it would be desirable, though, if the Apostolic See used the temporal goods in accordance with the patrimony of the institute. Although not explicitly mentioned in cc. 584 and 616 §2, it can be assumed that the Apostolic See must respect the intention of the founders and donors and acquired rights (see c. 123).

8. Erection and Suppression of Parts of Institutes of Consecrated Life (cc. 581, 585)

As a general principle, whatever concerns the institute as a whole is reserved to the Apostolic See or requires at least its approval. Whatever concerns parts of the institute (e.g., provinces or whatever name they are called by) belongs to the competent authority of the institute (see cc. 581, 585). This

[9] However, the suppression of the only house of an institute does not automatically entail the suppression of the entire institute. The institute as such could still have members and continue to exist. Even if the institute no longer has any members, it is only extinguished if it is legitimately suppressed by the competent authority or has ceased to act for a hundred years (see c. 120 §1).

includes erecting and suppressing parts, as well as joining those erected or redefining their boundaries. Who the competent authority of the institute is, is to be determined by the constitutions.[10] This could be the general chapter or the supreme moderator with his council.

9. Just Autonomy (c. 586)

A just autonomy of life, especially of governance, is acknowledged to all institutes of consecrated life (see c. 586). Just autonomy can be seen as a fundamental right of the institutes and employs the principle of subsidiarity. It includes the right to regulate their own affairs within the framework provided by universal law. Above all, just autonomy concerns the area of governance. This includes the autonomy to draw up a proper law for the institute (see c. 587).

Autonomy is restricted, for example, in the area of temporal goods and their administration. Religious institutes are capable of acquiring, possessing, administering, and alienating temporal goods (see c. 634 §1), but the pope has a right of supervision (see c. 1256), so that institutes are obliged to report on their finances in their periodic report to the Apostolic See (see c. 592 §1). In addition, the permission of the Apostolic See is required for certain financial transactions (see c. 638 §3). The temporal goods of institutes of consecrated life are ecclesiastical goods (see c. 1257 §1), so that the institutes are bound by the norms of cc. 1258–1310 on ecclesiastical temporal goods.

Just autonomy includes the right to decide whether or not to exercise an external apostolate. When exercising an external

[10] If the constitutions remain silent in this regard, the competence of the general chapter must be assumed in any case. See Apostolic Signatura, *Decretum definitivum* of 8 November 1997, Prot. N. 27013/96 CA; William L. Daniel, ed., *Ministerium Iustitiae: Jurisprudence of the Supreme Tribunal of the Apostolic Signatura* (Wilson & Lafleur, 2011), 287–98.

apostolate, the just autonomy of the institute is limited insofar as religious, in addition to their proper superiors, in this regard are also subject to the diocesan bishop (see c. 678 §1–2), who in his diocese is responsible for the coordination of all apostolic works and activities between the institutes and between the institutes and the diocese, while respecting the character and purpose of individual institutes and the laws of the foundation (see c. 680). *Mutuae Relationes* contains more detailed principles, guidelines, and norms in this regard, whereby the document on cooperation between bishops and religious is, at this writing, being revised.

The aim of the just autonomy granted to the institutes is to preserve their own patrimony intact. It is for local ordinaries to preserve and safeguard this autonomy (see c. 586 §2).

10. Constitutions and Proper Law (c. 587)

Just autonomy allows each institute to establish its own proper law within the framework provided by the universal law. This is intended to preserve the institute's own vocation and character faithfully. The Code distinguishes between two types of proper law: the fundamental law, or constitutions, and other norms.

a) Constitutions (c. 587 §§1–3)

The constitutions of an institute are rooted in its patrimony (see c. 578) and express the institute's own charism in the legal norms. They must contain the fundamental norms regarding governance of the institute, the discipline of members, incorporation and formation of members, and the proper object of the sacred bonds. In various norms of the Code, reference is made to the provisions in the constitutions, which must or can contain more detailed provisions on the legal matters in question:

Regarding all institutes of consecrated life:

- the establishment and rearrangement of parts of an institute (c. 581)
- the authority that superiors and chapters have over the members (c. 596 §1)
- the manner in which the evangelical counsels of chastity, poverty, and obedience must be observed (c. 598 §1)
- the scope of the vow of obedience (c. 601)

Regarding religious institutes:

- the erection of a house (c. 609 §1)
- the autonomy of a religious house of canons regular or of monks under the governance and care of its own moderator (c. 613 §1)
- the way of life and governance of monasteries of nuns associated to an institute of men or *sui iuris* (cc. 614–615)
- the suppression of a religious house (c. 616)
- the appointment or election of a major superior (c. 623)
- the term of office of the supreme moderator and of superiors of an autonomous house (c. 624 §1)
- the canonical election of the supreme moderator and appointment or election of other superiors (c. 625)
- the councils of superiors (c. 627 §1)
- the authority exercised by the general chapter, its composition and scope of authority (c. 631 §§1–2)
- the exclusion or restriction of the capacity of acquiring, possessing, administering, and alienating temporal goods of an institute, province, or house (c. 634 §1)
- periods of apostolic exercises to be spent outside the community of the novitiate (c. 648 §2)

- the institute's own way of the following of Christ (c. 662)
- cloister that is to be observed by monasteries of nuns (c. 667 §3)
- the dispositions regarding a member's goods before first profession (c. 668 §1)
- the responsibility of the institute to care for the members (c. 670)

Regarding secular institutes:

- the sacred bonds by which the evangelical counsels are assumed in the institute and obligations which these bonds bring about (c. 712)
- the way of life in the ordinary conditions of the world (c. 714)
- the proper manner of governance (c. 717 §1)
- admission into the institute (c. 720)
- impediments to admission (c. 721 §2)
- the manner and length of probation before taking first sacred bonds (c. 722 §3)
- provisions regarding first incorporation definitive incorporation (c. 723 §§2.4)
- formation after the first assumption of sacred bonds (c. 724 §1)
- the association of other members of the Christian faithful (c. 725)
- norms regarding seeking an indult of departure (c. 727 §1)
- causes for dismissal (c. 729)

Norms from other areas concerning institutes of consecrated life:

- permission for preaching to religious in their churches or oratories (c. 765)
- permission to publish writings dealing with questions of religion or morals (c. 832)
- the obligation to make a profession of faith of superiors in clerical religious institutes and societies of apostolic life (c. 833 n. 8)
- the faculty of hearing confession of superiors of religious institutes or societies of apostolic life that are clerical and of pontifical right (c. 968 §2)
- the granting of dimissorial letters for the diaconate and the presbyterate by major superiors of a clerical religious institute of pontifical right or of a clerical society of apostolic life of pontifical right (c. 1019 §1)
- the obligation to carry out the Liturgy of the Hours (c. 1174 §1)
- the order to reside in a certain place or territory (c. 1337 §1)
- the determination of the judge of first instance for controversies within the institute (c. 1427 §§1–2)

The enactment of constitutions and amendments to them is the responsibility of the competent authority of the institute, which is usually the general chapter. By their very nature, the constitutions have a certain permanence, so that changes to them should not be too frequent but can occur regularly if adaptations to changes in the Code of Canon Law are necessary or if the charism of the institute and thus also its patrimony, in which the constitutions are rooted, change.

Constitutions must be approved by the competent authority of the church and can only be changed with its consent. In the case of institutes of diocesan right, the competent authority is the bishop of the principal seat (see c. 595 §1), and in the case of institutes of pontifical right, it is the Apostolic See, in particular, the Dicastery for Institutes of Consecrated Life and Societies of Apostolic Life (see PE 124 §1, 1°).

Spiritual and juridical elements are to be joined together suitably in constitutions. This provision has its roots in the Second Vatican Council: "The union of both elements, spiritual and juridical, is necessary so that the principal codes of the institutes have a stable foundation and that the true spirit and life-giving norm pervade them; care must therefore be taken that a merely juridical or purely exhortatory text is not composed" (ES II,13).

Previously, constitutions were mere juridical texts. The inclusion of spiritual elements was not envisaged and was even explicitly forbidden for congregations with simple vows.[11] However, consecrated life cannot be defined in juridical terms only, so the inclusion of spiritual elements in constitutions is an important innovation. However, the question of how spiritual and juridical elements can be joined together suitably in constitutions is hardly dealt with in the relevant literature. One possible way is to divide the constitutions into two books, of which one contains the spiritual elements and the other the juridical elements.[12] This simple solution has the advantage

[11] See Sacra Congregatio de Religiosis, "Normae secundum quas Sacra Congregatio de Religiosis in novis religiosis congregationibus approbandis procedere solet," *AAS* 13 (1921): no. 22 (p. 317).

[12] This method is preferred, for example, by Josef F. Gallen, "Writing Constitutions," *RfR* 36 (1977): 773–87: "Some religious institutes prefer the interweaving of the spiritual with the juridical matter of the constitutions, which is certainly permitted and may even be the preferred way in the mind of the Roman Congregations. I have often stated and repeat here again that I prefer to separate these two classes of articles in the constitutions, the first section of which will then be spiritual and the second legal. My basic reason is that in the interweaving arrangement the juridical will try up the spiritual content" (779).

that the two different elements are not mixed up and each of the two books can use its own language. However, in this solution the spiritual and juridical elements are not joined together suitably but are deliberately kept separate. It is better to compose a single book of constitutions and include both elements in it.[13] The source for the spiritual elements is the patrimony (see c. 578), in which the constitutions are rooted. The legal elements are to protect the patrimony of an institute and ensure its practical implementation.[14] One approach may be to first name a spiritual element from the patrimony and then follow this up with legal norms for its protection and practical implementation. In this way, the patrimony of an institution is appropriately expressed in the legal elements.

Furthermore, the norms in the constitutions must not be multiplied needlessly (see c. 587 §3). The constitutions are the fundamental law of the institute and should therefore only contain those norms that must necessarily be included in them according to the Code of Canon Law. Firstly, it allows a certain flexibility if not too many details are rigidly regulated in the constitutions, leaving them to be regulated by the provinces or houses themselves or left to the decision of the superiors. Secondly, it has the practical advantage that norms can be

[13] This method is preferred, for example, by Miriam Cerletty, "Some Practical Helps for the Development of Constitutions," *StudCan* 14 (1980): 155–70: "In other words, there should be accurately formulated in the first book stable basic norms—doctrinal, juridical, inspirational—to define the identity of the Institute and the means to preserve that identity, and the purpose of the Institute and the means to further and attain that purpose. A combination of both elements, spiritual and juridical, is necessary so as to give a firm foundation to the particular law of the Institute and to ensure that it be permeated by a true spirit and an authentic rule of life. Care must be taken not to produce a text either purely juridical or merely exhortatory" (158).

[14] For further details, see Myriam Wijlens, "The Church Knowing and Acting: The Relationship Between Theology and Canon Law," *Louvain Studies* 20 (1995): 21–40.

changed without the approval of the competent authority of the church if they are not contained in the constitutions but in the other codes.

For a just and reasonable cause, the competent authority may dispense from the norms of the constitutions in individual cases (see c. 90 §1). In the case of institutes of diocesan right, the diocesan bishop is competent to dispense from the provisions of the constitutions (see c. 595 §2). This competence falls to both the bishop of the principal seat and the bishop of the place of the house to which the religious requesting the dispensation belongs (see c. 85). In clerical institutes of pontifical right, major superiors are ordinaries, so that they have the authority to dispense from the norms of the constitutions if it concerns their subjects. In any case, the Apostolic See can be approached for a dispensation.

b) Other Codes (c. 587 §4)

Constitutions are the fundamental law of an institute that contains the fundamental norms. They form a framework that is filled in by the other codes issued by the competent authority of the institute. This includes all norms issued by the general chapter and, if available, by the provincial chapter and conventual chapter, as well as by the competent superiors. These norms are to be collected suitably in other codes. Approval from an authority external to the institution is not required, but the norms in the other codes must not contradict the Code of Canon Law or the constitutions. The Code of Canon Law refers to the provisions of the institutes' proper law in various norms. In these cases, the institutes have the right to choose whether these matters are dealt with in the constitutions or in the other codes. The choice should generally fall on the latter option in order to have more flexibility in the event of amendments. A dispensation from the norms of other proprietary law is granted to the competent authority of the institute.

Further reading: Miriam Cerletty, "Some Practical Helps for the Development of Constitutions," *StudCan* 14 (1980): 155–70; Josef F. Gallen, "Writing Constitutions," *RfR* 36 (1977): 773–87; Joseph F. Gallen, "Guide for Conforming Constitutions to the New Code," *RfR* 42 (1983): 748–58; Yuji Sugawara, "Ruolo delle Costituzioni negli Istituti di vita consacrata," *PRC* 98 (2009): 663–91; Daniel Tibi, "L'adeguata armonizzazione degli elementi spirituali e giuridici nelle costituzioni (can. 587 § 3)," *QDE* 35 (2022): 82–90.

11. Typology (cc. 588–595)

The 1983 Code of Canon Law divides institutes of consecrated life into different types:

- clerical institutes and lay institutes
- institutes of pontifical right and institutes of diocesan right
- exempt institutes and non-exempt institutes

a) Clerical Institutes and Lay Institutes (c. 588)

The state of consecrated life is by its nature neither clerical nor lay (see c. 588 §1). An institute can be either clerical or lay by virtue of the design of the founder and its tradition. Due to the negative formulation in c. 588 §1, the question arises whether there can also be mixed or indifferent institutes, that is, institutes that are constituted in such a way that they are neither clerical nor lay.

aa) Clerical Institutes

An institute is clerical (see c. 588 §2), if

1. it is under the direction of clerics,
2. it assumes the exercise of sacred orders, and
3. it is recognized as such by the authority of the church.

The 1983 Code of Canon Law focuses on the actual orientation of an institute. The 1917 Code, on the other hand, made the distinction based on the number of clerics in the institute (see c. 488, 4° CIC/1917): a clerical institute was an institute in which most of the members were priests, otherwise it was lay. Major superiors of clerical institutes of pontifical right are ordinaries for their own members (see c. 134 §1). In the decree *Clericalia Instituta* of November 27, 1969,[15] the Congregation for Religious and Secular Institutes stipulated that lay members of clerical institutes could at the local, provincial, and general levels of governance be councilors, be appointed to administrative offices, and have active and passive voice at chapters, with the exception that they could not be superiors or vicars at any level of governance. In the course of the Second Vatican Council, there was a return to the idea of a fraternal equality of all members of an institute, regardless of whether they are ordained: "Men's monasteries and institutes which are not entirely lay can, of their nature, admit clerics and laymen, in accordance with the constitutions, on an equal footing and with equal rights and obligations, apart from those arising from sacred orders" (PC 15). As clerical institutes are under the direction of clerics, lay members, though, were still excluded from the office of a superior or vicar. In individual cases, the Apostolic See has in the past given permission that a lay member could exercise the office of a superior.[16] Those requests were dealt with on a case-by-case basis. On May 18, 2022, Pope Francis issued a rescript[17] that defined the procedure of

[15] Congregation for Religious and Secular Institutes, "Participation by Lay Religious in Government of Clerical Institutes," November 27, 1969, in *CLD* 7: 468–69.

[16] See, e.g., *CLD* 7: 467–71; *CLD* 8: 342–43; *CLD* 9: 341–46; *CLD* 10: 106–7.

[17] Pope Francis, "Rescriptum Ex Audientia Ss.Mi. Rescript of the Holy Father Francis Regarding the Derogation from Can. 588 § 2 CIC (18 May 2022)," *RRAO* 2022: 57.

appointing or electing a lay member as superior in a clerical institute. The wording of c. 588 §2 has not been changed. A lay member as superior in a clerical institute is still an exception and requires a legitimate reason. However, the rescript, in a way, institutionalized the exception and thus promoted it. The procedure is as follows:

1. A lay member is appointed as local superior (who is not an ordinary): The competent major superior with the consent of his council can appoint a lay member as local superior without the intervention of the Dicastery for Institutes of Consecrated Life and Societies of Apostolic Life.

2. A lay member is appointed as major superior: A lay member can be appointed as major superior by the supreme moderator with the consent of his council after having received written permission from the Dicastery for Institutes of Consecrated Life and Societies of Apostolic Life.

3. A lay member is elected major superior or supreme moderator: If a lay member has been duly elected major superior or supreme moderator, confirmation of the election through written approval from the Dicastery for Institutes of Consecrated Life and Societies of Apostolic Life is required.

In any case, if the intervention of the Dicastery for Institutes of Consecrated Life and Societies of Apostolic Life is required, it is up to the dicastery to examine in each individual case whether there is a legitimate reason.

Lay members who hold the office of a major superior or of a supreme moderator are not ordinaries.[18] Therefore, the proper law of the institute must determine who exercises the

[18] See Dicastery for Legislative Texts, "Risposta particolare," August 10, 2022, in *Comm* 54 (2022): 399–400. Ordinaries are major superiors who at least possess ordinary executive power (see c. 134 §1). However, only clerics can hold offices that require power of ecclesiastical governance (see c. 274 §1).

function of an ordinary in this case. This could be, for example, the vicar or, if there is one, the hierarchical superior within the institute.

Further reading: Pope Francis, "Rescriptum Ex Audientia Ss.Mi. Rescript of the Holy Father Francis Regarding the Derogation from Can. 588 § 2 CIC (18 May 2022)," *RRAO* 2022: 57; Ambroży Skorupa, "Participation of Religious Brothers in the Exercise of Authority in Clerical Religious Institutes," *KiP* 12 (2023): 201–14.

bb) Lay Institutes

According to the 1917 Code of Canon Law, lay institutes were all institutes that were not clerical (see c. 488 no. 4 CIC/1917). The 1983 Code, on the other hand, has a positive definition (see c. 588 §3). An institute is lay if it

1. is recognized as such by the authority of the church, and
2. has by virtue of its nature, character, and purpose a proper function defined by the founder or by tradition, that does not include the exercise of sacred orders.

Members of lay institutes work in areas that do not require the exercise of orders (e.g., social services, health care, and education), though some members may receive the orders for priestly service within the community. To avoid a confusion with the secular state of the lay faithful and to promote the spirituality behind the special way of living as brothers, *Vita Consecrata* 60 introduced the term "Religious Institutes of Brothers."[19]

[19] Pope John Paul II, Apostolic Exhortation *Vita Consecrata*, March 25, 1996 (hereafter, VC), https://www.vatican.va/content/john-paul-ii/en/apost_exhortations/documents/hf_jp-ii_exh_25031996_vita-consecrata.html.

Further reading: Congregation for Institutes of Consecrated Life and Societies of Apostolic Life, *Identity and Mission of the Religious Brother in the Church* (Libreria Editrice Vaticana, 2015).

cc) Mixed Institutes

The negative formulation in c. 588 §1 that the state of consecrated life is by its nature neither clerical nor lay, as well as the positive definitions of clerical and lay institutes in c. 588 §§2–3, opens up the possibility that there could be institutes that are neither clerical nor lay, but mixed (or indifferent). The wording of c. 588 neither explicitly provides for mixed institutes nor excludes them in principle. Mixed institutes are institutes "which in the founder's original design were envisaged as a brotherhood in which all the members, priests and those who were not priests, were considered equal among themselves, have acquired a different form with the passing of time" (VC 61). In particular, Benedictine and Franciscan communities come to mind, which only became clericalized in the course of their historical development. In other words, mixed institutes are institutes that assume the exercise of orders but that are not necessarily under the direction of clerics. In the course of the revision of the Code of Canon Law, the responsible commission voted on a proposal on March 2, 1979, according to which there should be clerical, lay, and indifferent institutes, and each institute could specify in its constitutions which type it was.[20] The proposal was rejected by a clear majority of two votes in favor and eight against. Therefore, the 1983 Code does not provide for mixed institutes. In *Vita Consecrata* 61, Pope John Paul II announced that a "special Commission has been established to examine and resolve the problems connected with this issue; it is necessary to await this Commission's conclusions before coming to suitable decisions in accordance

[20] See *Comm* 11 (1979): 61: "*Cuiuscumque Instituti est suis in Constitutionibus determinare utrum clericale sit vel laicale vel indifferens.*"

with what will be authoritatively determined." Until now, mixed institutes have not been officially recognized. However, the rescript of Pope Francis, which allows lay members to be superiors in exceptional cases, is a first step in this direction.

Further reading: Teodoro Bahíllo Ruiz, "Presencia de religiosos laicos en institutos clericales: institutos mixtos, ¿posibilidad real o vía sin salida?," *Estudios eclesiásticos* 89 (2014): 675–99; Takayoshi Noguchi, "La naturaleza clerical, laical y 'mixta' de los institutos religiosos del CIC 83," *Cuadernos doctorales* 20 (2003): 195–235.

b) Institutes of Pontifical Right and Institutes of Diocesan Right (cc. 589–590, 592–595)

After having been validly erected by the diocesan bishop (see c. 579), the new institute is an institute of diocesan right. It retains this status until it has received a formal decree of approval from the Apostolic See, whereby it becomes an institute of pontifical right (see c. 589). An institute erected directly by the Apostolic See becomes an institute of pontifical law upon its erection, although this is the exception in practice.

All institutes of consecrated life, those of diocesan right as well as those of pontifical right, are subject to the supreme authority of the church in a special way (see c. 590 §1), because institutes are dedicated in a special way to the service of the whole church. The supreme authority of the church is the pope and the college of bishops (see cc. 330–331). With regard to institutes of diocesan right, this results in a cumulative competence of the diocesan bishop and the Apostolic See.[21]

[21] Apostolic Signatura, *Decretum definitivum* of 24 June 2014, Prot. N. 47546/13 CA, *PRC* 112 (2023): 101–23. "*Instituta insuper speciali curae Episcopi dioecesani commissa minime subtrahuntur Supremae Ecclesiae auctoritati, uti cavet ipse Legislator: 'Instituta vitae consecratae supremae eiusdem [= Ecclesiae] auctoritati peculiari ratione subduntur' (can. 590, § 1). Competentia ergo Episcopi, sedis quoque principalis, illi cumulatur quae a Sede Apostolica exercetur.*"

Members of institutes of consecrated life are bound to obey the pope as their highest superior by reason of the sacred bond of obedience (see c. 590 §2). This applies only to the pope himself and not to the dicasteries of the Apostolic See.

Two legal obligations arise from the special relationship of all institutes of consecrated life to the supreme authority of the church (see c. 592):

1. to periodically send a brief report of the state and life of the institute to the Apostolic See; and
2. to promote knowledge of documents of the Apostolic See which regard the members of the institutes to take care about their observance.

The periodic report is to be sent by the supreme moderator of an institute to the Dicastery for Institutes of Consecrated Life and Societies of Apostolic Life at the time of the general chapter. The dicastery issued the following guidelines for the report:

1. FOUNDATION, CHARISM, AND MISSION OF THE INSTITUTE (cf. *Vita consecrata* 36–37)

Provide a brief description of the identity of the Institute and of the aspects of the founding Charism which were most stressed in recent years.

2. A BRIEF AND SUMMARIZED STATISTICAL REPORT (cf. *Vita consecrata* 40)

Members

- Number of perpetually professed members with age distribution.
- Number of temporarily professed members with age distribution.
- Number of *formandi* in each level of formation, divided by continent of origin.

- Distribution of members according to Continents.
- Number of departures and primary reasons.

Houses/Regions/Provinces/Delegations/Zones

- Number and divisions according to Continents.

3. CONSTITUTIONS, RULES, AND CUSTOMS OF THE INSTITUTE (cf. *Vita consecrata* 36–37; 68)

- Date of the latest approved revision of the Constitutions?
- Are the Constitutions presently in need of revision?
- When was the *Ratio institutionis* last revised?
- What means are used in ongoing formation to assist members in their knowledge of and fidelity to the Constitution and Rules of the Institute?

4. THE PRIMACY OF THE SPIRIT (cf. *Vita consecrata* 17–19; 35; 39; 88–90)

- What are some tangible signs of the members' desire to respond to the call to holiness through the *sequela Christi* and the living of Gospel values?
- Describe the members' commitment to Liturgy, the Word, and personal prayer as responses to the Spirit's promptings to be configured to Christ.

5. COMMUNION IN COMMUNITY (cf. *Vita consecrata* 41–45; 69–71)

- Do the members manifest an appreciation of Consecrated life, lived as *signum fraternitatis*?
- Do they give witness to being communities rich in "joy and the Holy Spirit" (Acts 13:52)?
- How much emphasis is placed on *lectio divina*, faith-sharing, and community meetings, etc.?

- How much importance is placed upon "life lived in common" and the spiritual and human growth of individual members?
- How are elderly members cared for? What means are taken to form new leadership?
- How is authority exercised within the Institute at the various levels (Houses, Regions, Provinces, etc.) and what means are used to facilitate communication and relationships among the various levels?

6. MISSION AND MINISTRY
(cf. *Vita consecrata* 72–83; 96–99)

- How do members manifest their appreciation of Consecrated Life lived in the Church as *servitum caritatis*?
- In what ministries are members of the community currently involved and how do these ministries reflect the founding charism in the various Cultures where members serve?
- What programs of ongoing formation are offered to members in order to assure an updated and inculturated apostolic spirituality?
- In the light of internal demographic shifts, what measures are being employed by the Institute to respond to its mission in the Church?
- How is the Institute responding to new needs in the mission and the world?

7. VOCATION RECRUITMENT/FORMATION
(cf. *Vita consecrata* 63–71)

- When were the *Ratio formationis* and the *Ratio studiorum* last revised?
- What means are taken to recruit new members?

- What criteria are used in the selection and retention of new members?
- How are members formed in the Institute?
- Does the Institute form part of any Inter-Institute formation program?

8. RELATIONS IN THE CHURCH
(cf. *Vita consecrata* 45; 52–53)

- How are members formed in the spirituality of communion, in *sentire cum Ecclesia*, in insertion of communities into the Dioceses in which they serve, relationships with Bishops and Pastors?
- Does the Institute form part of any Federations or Unions of Institutes with similar Charisms (cf. can. 582)?
- Is the Institute a member of the International and National Conferences of Superiors General?

9. FINANCIAL STATUS AND PROPERTIES
(cf. *Vita consecrata* 89–90)

- What is the status of the Institute's finances and properties?
- Is the community able to support its missions and members?
- What provisions are made for the sharing of goods within the Institute and for the medical and retirement care of the members?
- What initiatives does the Institute undertake to share its goods with the poor?

10. STATUS OF THE INSTITUTE
(cf. *Vita consecrata* 84–95)

- What are the major successes and challenges which the Institute has experienced in recent years?

- What are the major issues which the Institute must confront during the next administration?
- What are the short and long range plans for the future of the Institute?
- Other questions of particular interest.[22]

Further reading: Rose McDermott, "Fostering Communion Between the Apostolic See and Religious Institutes and Societies of Apostolic Life: 2008 Guidelines for the Report in Canon 592 §1," *Jur* 72 (2012): 428–52.

aa) Institutes of Diocesan Right (cc. 594–595)

An institute of diocesan right remains under the special care of the diocesan bishop (see c. 594), without prejudice to its just autonomy (see c. 586 §1). According to c. 492 §2 of the 1917 Code, institutes of diocesan right were fully subject to the jurisdiction of the diocesan bishop. The 1983 Code, however, emphasizes their due autonomy. The diocesan bishop is the ecclesiastical superior of an institute of diocesan right and its members, but not the hierarchical superior. This means that the vow of obedience does not include obedience to the diocesan bishop.[23]

[22] Congregation for Institutes of Consecrated Life and Societies of Apostolic Life (hereafter, CICLSAL), "Suggested Guidelines for the Preparation of Periodic Reports on the Status and Life of Institutes of Consecrated Life and Societies of Apostolic Life," May 11, 2008, Prot. N. SpR 640/2008, in *Studies in Church Law* 5 (2009): 41–44. Also available at https://www.vatican.va/roman_curia/congregations/ccscrlife/documents/rc_con_ccscrlife_doc_20080511_relazione-periodica_en.html.

[23] See *Comm* 18 (1986): 199: "*Instituta enim pendent ab Episcopo, non autem qua Superiore religioso interno, sed qua superiore ecclesiastico. Religiosi votum nuncupant oboedientiae ad superiores internos, non autem ad Episcopum.*" The Apostolic Signatura confirmed this. See also Apostolic Signatura, *Decretum definitivum* of 24 June 2014, Prot. N. 47546/13 CA, *PRC* 112 (2023): 101–23.

In particular, it is up to the diocesan bishop

- to grant dispensations from the constitutions in particular cases (see c. 595 §2);
- to carry out the canonical visitation in individual houses of an institute of diocesan right located in his own territory (see c. 628 §2, 2°);
- to be informed about the financial reports of a religious house of diocesan right (see 637);
- to give written consent for certain financial transactions, required for validity (see c. 638 §4);
- to grant an indult of exclaustration to a religious professed by perpetual vows, except nuns, but not for more than five years (see c. 686 §1);
- to impose exclaustration on a religious, except nuns, at the petition of the supreme moderator with the consent of his council (see c. 686 §3); and
- to issue an indult of departure for a perpetually professed religious (see c. 691 §2).

The diocesan bishop of the principal seat of an institute has a special role. In particular, it is up to him

- to approve the constitutions and confirm changes legitimately introduced into them (see c. 595 §1);
- to treat affairs of greater importance affecting the whole institute which exceed the power of internal authority, after he has, for validity (see c. 127 §2, 2°), consulted the other diocesan bishops, if the institute has spread over several dioceses (see c. 595 §1)[24]; and

[24] Compared to the 1917 Code, there was one small but significant change: According to the previous Code (see c. 495 §2), the bishop of the principal seat needed the consent of each of the bishops, which could prove difficult in practice. Now only consultation is required.

- to preside at the election of the supreme moderator (see c. 625 §2).

Further reading: Rose McDermott, "The Vigilance of the Diocesan or Eparchial Bishop: Diocesan / Eparchial Right Institutes / Sui iuris Monasteries / Hermits / Ascetics / Virgins / Widows," *Studies in Church Law* 8 (2012): 141–74.

bb) Institutes of Pontifical Right (cc. 592–593)

All institutes of consecrated life are subject to the supreme authority of the church in a special way (see c. 590 §1). In addition, institutes of pontifical right are immediately and exclusively subject to the power of the Apostolic See in regard to internal governance and discipline, without prejudice to their due autonomy (see c. 593). Institutes of pontifical right are therefore removed from the authority of the diocesan bishop and are directly subordinate to the Apostolic See, though with some exceptions. A bishop can visit members of religious institutes of pontifical right and their houses only in the cases expressed in law (see c. 397 §2). Canon 683 §1 includes such an exception: At the time of pastoral visitation and in the case of necessity, the diocesan bishop can, though is not obliged to, visit churches and oratories of religious institutes that the Christian faithful habitually attend, and schools and other works of religion or charity, whether spiritual or temporal, entrusted to religious, but not schools which are open exclusively to the institute's own students. Furthermore, religious are subject to the diocesan bishop in matters that regard the care of souls, the public exercise of divine worship, and other works of the apostolate (see c. 678 §1), as all the works and apostolic activities in a diocese are under the direction of the diocesan bishop (see c. 680).

Though an institute of consecrated life can be erected directly by the Apostolic See, institutes are usually initially erected by a diocesan bishop with written permission of the

Apostolic See as an institute of diocesan right. If the new foundation consolidates over time, so that the institute spreads across several dioceses and the number of members increases, the status of an institute of pontifical right can be applied for from the Apostolic See. At such time, the following requirements must be met and the following documents must be submitted to the Dicastery for Institutes of Consecrated Life and Societies of Apostolic Life:

1. Historical and legal report on the institute from its beginnings. A copy of the decree by which the competent bishop erected the institute must be attached. The report must contain the following points in particular:
   a) name of the founder; purpose of the foundation; date and place of the beginning; name of the diocesan bishop who authorized the new foundation
   b) number and names of the first members
   c) construction, date, and location of the first novitiate house; name of the bishop who authorized the building of the novitiate house; number of first novices and the date of their admission to the novitiate; number of candidates and the date of their first profession; name of the director of novices; names of those other than the director of novices who were responsible for the initial formation of the first members
   d) dates of the general chapters held
   e) name of the diocesan bishop who approved the first constitutions
   f) apostolic activity of the association at the beginning and in the present
   g) expansion of the association to other dioceses
   h) spirituality of the association

For clerical institutes: indication where those preparing to receive ordination are trained

2. Curriculum vitae of the founder of the institute: name, date, and place of birth and baptism; names of parents; education; other important events in his or her life.

3. Curriculum vitae of the first superior general of the institute: in addition to the above-mentioned information: date of entry into the institute and of temporary and perpetual profession; date of appointment or election as superior general; modalities of appointment or election and term of office; current circumstances of life. If the founder and the first superior general were members of another religious institute: beginning of novitiate, date of temporary and perpetual profession in that institute and ordination to the priesthood (if a priest). What authorization did they have to proceed with the foundation?

4. At least ten years must have passed since the erection as institute of diocesan right.

5. It might be necessary to have a representative or house in Rome.

6. Statistics of members and houses: names of temporary and perpetual professed, priests, novices, and postulants; age of professed and priests; number of candidates and date of the next temporary and perpetual profession; number of houses in which the members live; names of the dioceses in which the institute is present. The recognition as an institute of pontifical right requires at least one hundred professed members, the majority of whom must have taken perpetual vows.

7. Financial report: amount of debt; amount of funds deposited with banks (if possible in US$ or euros); number of properties owned by the association.

8. Statements on whether there have been any unusual events, such as visions or similar, and whether there is another Institute with the same name or the same charism in the diocese of the principal seat.

9. Description of the habit.

10. Ten copies of the current constitutions and of the directory.

11. Letters of recommendation from all the diocesan bishops concerned, including the bishop of the principal seat, to be sent directly to the dicastery and containing statements on the following points:
    a) Usefulness and stability of the association.
    b) Discipline of the members.
    c) Liturgy and administration of the sacraments.
    d) Attitude towards the church and collaboration with the ecclesiastical authority.
    e) Initial and further formation.
    f) Financial management.
    g) Ability to take responsibility for the management of an institute that is present internationally.

12. If possible, a deposit of €500 to be paid to the cash office of the Dicastery for Institutes of Consecrated Life and Societies of Apostolic Life, which will be cleared at the end of the procedure.[25]

Further reading: Javier Gonzalez, "From Diocesan to Pontifical Right: The Shifting of a Religious Institute," *Philippine Canonical Forum* 11 (2009): 259–69; Rudolf Henseler,"Vom

[25] See Rudolf Henseler, "Vom institutum iuris diocesani zum institutum iuris pontificii: Die zwölf Erfordernisse," in *Veritas vos liberabit*, ed. Matthias Pulte (Schöningh, 2017), 481–90.

institutum iuris diocesani zum institutum iuris pontificii: Die zwölf Erfordernisse," in *Veritas vos liberabit*, ed. Matthias Pulte (Schöningh, 2017), 481–90.

c) Exempt and Non-Exempt Institutes (c. 591)

Historically, religious exemption meant that a religious institute was excluded from the jurisdiction of the local bishop and was made subject directly to the pope, so that the institute could carry out its work and apostolate more freely and effectively. According to the 1917 Code of Canon Law, all male religious orders (i.e., all religious institutes where solemn vows were made) and all of their members, including novices, were exempt by virtue of the law itself, as were female religious orders that were subject to a male religious superior (see c. 615). Not exempt by virtue of the law itself were religious congregations (i.e., religious institutes where only simple vows were made) and their members, but exemption could be granted to them by decree of the Apostolic See (see c. 618 §1). In the 1983 Code of Canon Law, there is no more an exemption by virtue of the law itself. If exemption has been granted to an institute by decree of the Apostolic See before the 1983 Code came into force, the privilege of exemption remains intact if it has not been revoked (see c. 4). The current Code still offers the possibility that the pope "can exempt institutes of consecrated life from the governance of local ordinaries and subject them to himself alone or to another ecclesiastical authority" in order to "provide better for the good of institutes and the needs of the apostolate" (c. 591). Exemption, also in the new Code, usually means to remove an institute from the jurisdiction of the local bishop and make it subject directly to the pope. To make it subject to another ecclesiastical authority would be possible but is not common.[26] According to the 1983

[26] It would be possible, for example, to remove a religious institute of nuns from the jurisdiction of the bishop and make it subject to a male religious superior.

Code, all institutes enjoy a due autonomy of life and governance, and the level of subordination under the local bishop depends on whether the institute is of diocesan or pontifical right. "Therefore, it is difficult to explain the nature of exempt institutes. There seems little distinction between exempt clerical institutes and clerical institutes of pontifical right."[27] In general, religious exemption refers to the internal order of an institute: "The institute of exemption, by which Religious are called to the service of the supreme pontiff or other ecclesiastical authority and withdrawn from the jurisdiction of bishops, refers chiefly to the internal order of their communities so that in them all things may be properly coordinated and the growth and perfection of the Religious common life promoted."[28] Regarding works of the apostolate and the public exercise of divine worship, all institutes remain under the authority of the bishop (see c. 678 §§1–2; CD 35, 4°). In practice, the institute of exemption is therefore only of minor importance, and was, generally speaking, replaced by the institute of due autonomy (see c. 593).

Further reading: John M. Huels, "The Demise of Religious Exemption," *Jur* 54 (1994): 40–55; David J. Kay, *Exemption: Origins of Exemption and Vatican Council II* (Editrice Pontificia Università Gregoriana, 1990).

12. Superiors and Chapters (c. 596)

Superiors and chapters of all levels of an institute (general, provincial, and local) possess that power over members that is defined in universal law and in the constitutions (see c. 596 §1). The scope of their power can vary from institute to institute.

[27] Rose M. McDermott, "Title I: Norms Common to All Institutes of Consecrated Life [cc. 573–606]," in *New Commentary on the Code of Canon Law*, ed. John P. Beal et al. (Paulist, 2000), 759.

[28] Second Vatican Council, Decree on the Pastoral Office of Bishops in the Church *Christus Dominus*, October 28, 1965 (hereafter, CD), no. 35, 3°.

Universal law deals with the power of superiors and chapters of religious institutes in cc. 617–633. The constitutions regulate further details. The proper manner of governance of a secular institute is to be prescribed in its constitutions (see c. 717 §1).

The power referred to in c. 596 §1 is not defined in the Code. However, a distinction can be made between the following types of power. All superiors have domestic power (*potestas domestica*). That is the power to regulate everyday life and to provide the order in the institute, province, or house. In addition, all superiors are entrusted with the care of their subordinates. The 1917 Code called this power dominative power (*potestas dominativa*, c. 501 §1 CIC/1917). Though the 1983 Code does not use this term, it still can be used to describe the power all superiors have over subordinates. Dominative power has a private law character, but, because it includes the exercise of power in the name of the church—for example, admission to the novitiate and to profession, and in some cases granting an indult of exclaustration or departure—it has a certain public law character, and acts placed by religious superiors (even lay superiors) in regard to their subordinates are to be considered as acts of administrative power.[29] The prescripts of cc. 131, 133, and 137–144, that mainly deal with delegation and supplementation, apply to dominative power (see c. 596 §3). Superiors and chapters of clerical religious institutes of pontifical right furthermore possess ecclesiastical power of governance for both the external and internal forum (see c. 596 §2). Major superiors of clerical religious institutes of pontifical right that are clerics are ordinaries for their own members (see c. 134 §1).

[29] This means that controversies between a religious superior and a subordinate are always to be brought before the superior by means of an administrative recourse or before an administrative tribunal, even if the superior is a lay person. See Apostolic Signatura, *Litterae* of February 9, 1988, Prot. N. 19764/88 VT, in Beal et al., *New Commentary*, 1823.

Further reading: Julio García Martín, "La potestad de los superiores religiosos de los institutos religiosos laicales de derecho pontificio," *CpRM* 85 (2004): 31–75; Isaias Antonio Tiongco, "La Naturaleza de la Potestad en los Institutos Religiosos a la luz de las Codificaciones de 1917 y de 1983," *Philippiniana Sacra* 46 (2011): 3–29.

13. Basic Requirements for Admission (c. 597)

The basic requirements for admission into an institute of consecrated life are (see c. 597 §1):

- being a Catholic,
- having right intention,
- possessing the qualities required by universal law and proper law, and
- having no impediments.

Any Catholic—that is, anyone who was baptized in the Catholic Church or who came into full communion with the Catholic Church after baptism in another Christian church or ecclesial community—can be admitted. In addition, they must not have defected notoriously from the Catholic faith, as this is a reason for an ipso facto dismissal from an institute (see c. 694 §1,1°) and, vice versa, means that admission is not possible.

Furthermore, a person who seeks admission must be endowed with a right intention. They must strive for religious life, as outlined in c. 573 §1, according to the patrimony of the institute, for its own sake and not just as a means to an end (for example, to be materially secure). This point needs special attention during the discernment process.

Canon 597 §1 lists only the basic requirements for admission. Further requirements for admission into a religious institute are to be found in cc. 641–645, and further requirements for admission into a secular institute are to be found in cc. 720–721. Additional requirements may be specified in the proper law of the institute.

Not least, there must not be any impediments. Impediments for valid admission into a religious institute are listed in c. 643, and impediments for the valid admission into a secular institute are listed in c. 721. Proper law (for religious institutes) or the constitutions (for secular institutes) can establish other impediments even for validity of admission or can attach conditions.

No one can be admitted into an institute of consecrated life without suitable preparation (see c. 597 §2). The nature, structure, and duration of this pre-novitiate formation is not regulated by universal law and is therefore to be determined by the proper law of the institutes. Traditionally, the pre-novitiate formation consists of candidacy and postulancy. The candidacy is a time in which the candidate and the institute get to know each other, and the candidate deepens their understanding and experience of the charism of the institute. Candidates normally remain in their usual environment and come for longer visits to houses of the institute where they live, pray, and work with the members. During the time of candidacy, a deepening of human and religious formation may take place, depending on the needs of each individual candidate. Postulants usually move into a house of the institute, though they do not yet become a member of the institute. This increases the opportunity to get to know each other. For nuns, *Cor Orans* 262–276 contains more detailed provisions regarding candidacy (which the document refers to as "aspirancy") and postulancy. Both stages of pre-novitiate formation are compulsory for prospective nuns. The aspirancy and the postulancy each have a minimum duration of twelve months, and each stage may be extended in an individual case according to need at the discretion of the major superior (abbess or prioress), after having consulted her council, but for no longer than two years each (see CO 268).

Further reading: Nancy Bauer, "The Lengthening Duration of Initial Formation in Religious Institutes: Historical-Canonical Overview," *StudCan* 55 (2021): 147–67.

14. The Evangelical Counsels (cc. 598–601)

The evangelical counsels of chastity, poverty, and obedience are an essential element of consecrated life (see c. 573). By means of vows (in religious institutes) or other sacred bonds (in secular institutes), the evangelical counsels and the obligations they entail are assumed. Only the basic principles of the evangelical councils, which apply to all institutes, are dealt with in universal law (see cc. 599–601). The manner in which the evangelical counsels must be observed is rooted in the patrimony of an institute and is to be defined in its constitutions (see c. 598 §1).[30] The evangelical counsels of poverty and obedience can take different forms according to the patrimony of an institute. In the case of the evangelical counsel of chastity, there is no leeway. The members of an institute must faithfully and fully observe the evangelical counsels and live according to the proper law of their institute, thus striving for perfection of their state (see c. 598 §2).

According to the Second Vatican Council, the evangelical counsel of chastity, to which members of institutes of consecrated life commit themselves, "is a special symbol of heavenly benefits" and is "for religious . . . a most effective way of dedicating themselves whole-heartedly to the divine service and the works of the apostolate" (PC 12). It entails the obligation of perfect continence in celibacy (see c. 599). A public perpetual

[30] In the constitutions, a clear definition of each vow or sacred bond is required. In terms of language, it is advisable not to define them exclusively in terms of prohibitions but also to include and emphasize positive elements.

vow of chastity in a religious institute is a diriment impediment to marriage (see c. 1088). One who is bound by such a vow cannot enter into a valid marriage.[31] An attempt would lead to the dismissal ipso facto from the institute (see c. 694 §1, 2°) and to ecclesiastical penalties (see c. 1394). Other violations of the evangelical counsel of chastity are also subject to ecclesiastical penalties (see cc. 695–696; 729).

The evangelical counsel of poverty can be expressed in many ways, according to the patrimony of an institute (see c. 600). It is an expression of the following of Christ; therefore, "religious should be poor in fact and in spirit, having their treasures in heaven" (PC 13). The evangelical counsel of poverty should always include a certain simplicity of lifestyle and a certain dependence on the congregation and the superiors regarding temporal goods. The basic principles of how poverty is lived in an institute should be laid down in the constitutions. In religious institutes, c. 668 must also be observed. In secular institutes, their secular way of life has to be taken into account. The proper law may determine further details, like personal allowances, travel expenses, gifts, and so on.

The evangelical counsel of obedience means "the submission of the will to legitimate superiors, who stand in the place of God, when they command according to the proper constitutions" (c. 601). It is a sacrifice of one's own will to God (see PC 14). Superiors thus have a mediating function. They are to reflect the will of God in their commands. The will of God is manifested especially in common search and dialogue within the community (see VC 92), emphasizing the element of mutual obedience of all members of an institute. The final decision, after a preliminary dialogue, is generally left to the superior, though in certain cases the superior is required to

[31] This does not apply to a person who has taken temporary vows in a religious institute or to a member of a secular institute. In these cases, a marriage would be illicit but valid and would lead to the dismissal ipso facto from the institute (see cc. 694 §1, 2°; 729).

consult his or her council first or even to obtain his or her council's permission. The obligation to obey superiors is not absolute but applies only when superiors give commands within the scope of the constitutions (see c. 601). The scope of the superior's authority is, therefore, to be defined in the constitutions. A superior may not give commands that are contrary to natural law, divine positive law, universal law, or the constitutions and the proper law of the institute. The evangelical counsel of obedience is binding only towards legitimate superiors and their vicars. As a matter of principle, it does not include the officials (e.g., finance officer) of the institute, unless otherwise determined by the constitutions. With regard to institutes of diocesan right and their members, the diocesan bishop is an ecclesiastical superior but not a hierarchical superior, so that the evangelical counsel of obedience does not bind towards him.[32] By reason of the sacred bond of obedience, members of institutes of consecrated life are bound to obey the pope as their highest superior (see c. 590 §2). This obligation extends only to the pope personally and not to the dicasteries of the Apostolic See.

Further reading: Nancy Bauer, "Three Perspectives on Obedience: Benedict of Nursia, Ignatius of Loyola and the 1983 Code of Canon Law," *Jur* 65 (2005): 55–97; Sharon A. Euart, "Religious Institutes and the Juridical Relationship of the Members to the Institute," *Jur* 51 (1991): 103–18; Astrid Kaptijn, "Submission of the Will and Violation of the Vow of Obedience: Contributions to the Discussion of Canon 601," *Jur* 56 (1996): 307–37; Rose McDermott, "Stewards of Gifts to Be Shared:

[32] See *Comm* 18 (1986): 199: "*Instituta enim pendent ab Episcopo, non autem qua Superiore religioso interno, sed qua superiore ecclesiastico. Religiosi votum nuncupant oboedientiae ad superiores internos, non autem ad Episcopum.*" The Apostolic Signatura confirmed this. See also Apostolic Signatura, *Decretum definitivum* of June 24, 2014, Prot. N. 47546/13 CA, *PRC* 112 (2023): 101–23.

The Vow of Poverty in Religious Life," *Studies in Church Law* 3 (2007): 95–128; Rosemary Smith, "The Personal Patrimony of Individual Members of Religious Institutes: Current Issues," *CLSA Proceedings* 62 (2000): 263–81; Yuji Sugawara, *Religious Poverty: From Vatican Council II to the 1994 Synod of Bishops*, Tesi Gregoriana / Serie Diritto Canonico 3 (Pontificia Università Gregoriana, 1997).

15. Communion of Life (c. 602)

The members of institutes of consecrated life share a communion of life (see c. 602), "after the example of the early church, in which the company of believers was of one heart and mind" (PC 15). The purpose of this communion of life is mutual support and assistance in the fulfillment of one's vocation. Only members of religious institutes are obliged to live in community, that is, in their own religious house (see c. 665 §1). Members of secular institutes share a communion of life but do not live in community in a religious house. Secular institutes practice communion of life especially in the form of regular meetings and mutual support.

16. Other Forms of Consecrated Life (cc. 603–605)

The Code of Canon Law recognizes other forms of consecrated life (see cc. 603–605) besides institutes of consecrated life. These include

- diocesan hermits (see c. 603),
- consecrated virgins (see c. 604), and
- new forms of consecrated life (see c. 605).

The Code of Canon Law does not recognize consecrated widows, as the Code of Canons of the Eastern Churches does (see c. 570 CCEO). However, the consecration of widows is also practiced in the Latin Catholic Church.

Further reading: Peter O. Akpoghiran, *The Catholic Formulary in Accordance with the Code of Canon Law*, vol. 7a: *Eremitical and Order of Virgins Acts* (CreateSpace, 2020); Amy Hereford, *See I Am Making Something New: A Canonical and Pastoral Guidebook on New Institutes, Diocesan Hermits and Consecrated Virgins and New Forms of Consecrated Life* (CreateSpace, 2018); Rose McDermott, "The Vigilance of the Diocesan or Eparchial Bishop: Diocesan / Eparchial Right Institutes / Sui iuris Monasteries / Hermits / Ascetics / Virgins / Widows," *Studies in Church Law* 8 (2012): 141–74; Sean O. Sheridan, "Consecrated Virgins and Hermits," *Jur* 73 (2013): 493–512.

a) Diocesan Hermits (c. 603)

The eremitical life has a long tradition. Throughout history, the cenobitic monastic life has prevailed, but the Catholic Church also recognizes orders that combine the eremitical life with elements of the cenobitic life, such as the Camaldolese and the Carthusians. In addition, some cenobitic monastic orders provide in their proper law for the possibility of a member living as a hermit. In this case, the religious remains a member of their institute and continues to be subject to their religious superior. There are also persons who live as hermits without having taken public vows. In the absence of a public commitment to the evangelical counsels, they are not considered consecrated in the sense of canon law. In addition to these forms, the Code of Canon Law of 1983 recognizes another possibility of the eremitical life that did not previously exist in canon law: the diocesan hermit.

A diocesan hermit commits themself to the three evangelical counsels in a public vow or other sacred bond (see c. 603 §2)[33] and is, therefore, a form of consecrated life. The vow or other sacred bond is received by the diocesan bishop

[33] On sacred bonds, see Melanie S. Reyes, "A Comparative Study of Sacred Bonds in Institutes of Consecrated Life," *Philippiniana Sacra* 54 (2019): 219–40.

in the name of the church. The diocesan hermit is thus under the direction of the diocesan bishop. There are no other norms in the Code of Canon Law concerning a diocesan hermit. On September 14, 2002, the Congregation for Institutes of Consecrated Life and Societies of Apostolic Life published guidelines entitled *The Hermit's Way of Life in the Local Church*, which, after a theological section, also contains information that is legally relevant.

A candidate should not be admitted without prior examination and preparation for the eremitical life. Since there are no norms specifically for diocesan hermits, cc. 641–645 on the admission of candidates into religious institutes can be applied by analogy. Alternatively, specific diocesan guidelines may be established. This is left to the discretion of each diocesan bishop. Candidates should be in good health, of suitable character, and of sufficient psycho-affective maturity. In addition, candidates should be free of debts and other civil, criminal, or ecclesiastical liabilities. If the candidate is a member of an institute of consecrated life or a society of apostolic life, an indult of exclaustration is required for the probationary period and an indult of departure is required before the definitive commitment as a diocesan hermit. A diocesan priest may be admitted as a diocesan hermit by the bishop of the diocese in which he is incardinated. Candidates should address the questions of their motivation and experience in the contemplative life, their personal biography, and, not least, their economic situation. A diocesan hermit, if not a diocesan priest, is not entitled to support from the bishop and must earn their own living, usually through a professional activity compatible with their eremitical way of life. The income should be sufficient not only for a modest living but also for social security and retirement. Therefore, it may be necessary to first find a job, possibly part-time, that is compatible with the eremitical lifestyle and provides enough money to support one's life as a diocesan hermit and one's own social security. Before making a lifelong commitment as a diocesan hermit, there should be a sufficient probationary period, similar to the novitiate and temporary profession in religious institutes.

In accordance with the eremitical tradition, the diocesan hermit draws up their own rule of life and submits it to the diocesan bishop for approval. At least the following points should be dealt with in the rule of life:

- manner in which the evangelical counsels of chastity, poverty, and obedience must be observed
- accountability to the bishop regarding financial administration
- nature of the relationship with the bishop
- duration of lawful absence from the hermitage
- nature of the integration into the diocese
- norms for the reception of guests in the hermitage
- cases in that the bishop's permission is required

The rule of life must be in accordance with canon law, the teachings of the church, and the tradition of the eremitical life. It should reflect a realistic balance between ideal and reality. The rule of life should first be approved *ad experimentum* and tested for some time to ensure its suitability for practice. As time goes on, changes may become necessary, requiring the approval of the diocesan bishop.

The public profession of the evangelical counsels takes the form of a vow or other sacred bond. The form and content, as well as the liturgical celebration, are agreed upon by the hermit and the bishop. The rule of life drawn up by the hermit and approved by the bishop is part of the commitment made.

After having made a lifelong commitment, a hermit may wish to move to another diocese or to abandon the eremitical life, or the bishop might need to dismiss the hermit. The Code of Canon Law does not provide for these cases. The guidelines of the Congregation for Institutes of Consecrated Life and

Societies of Apostolic Life contain the following provisions for these cases: A transfer to another diocese requires the consent of the hermit and both bishops involved.[34] If a diocesan hermit wishes to abandon the eremitical life, the diocesan bishop may, for serious reasons, grant a dispensation from the vows or bonds by analogous application of cc. 691–692. Likewise, the diocesan bishop may, for grave reasons, dismiss a diocesan hermit by analogous application of cc. 691–704, or declare his dismissal ipso facto by analogous application of c. 694.

Further reading: Brian T. Austin, "Canon 603: Transfer of a Diocesan Hermit or Hermitess," *RRAO* 2020: 114–17; Congregation for Institutes of Consecrated Life and Societies of Apostolic Life, *The Hermit's Way of Life in the Local Church* (Libreria Editrice Vaticana, 2022); Helen MacDonald, "Hermits: The Juridical Implications of Canon 603," *StudCan* 26 (1992): 163–90.

b) Consecrated Virgins (c. 604)

The Code of Canon Law mentions consecrated virgins, "who, expressing the holy resolution of following Christ more closely, are consecrated to God by the diocesan bishop according to the approved liturgical rite" (c. 604 §1) as a form of the consecrated life. Whether consecrated virgins actually belong to the consecrated life is disputed in canonical literature, since they limit themselves to the profession of chastity and thus do not commit themselves to all three evangelical counsels. However, the apostolic constitution *Praedicate Evangelium* includes consecrated virgins among the forms of consecrated life.[35] The *ordo virginum* has a long tradition, dating back to the early

[34] See also Brian T. Austin, "Canon 603: Transfer of a Diocesan Hermit or Hermitess," *RRAO* 2020: 114–17.

[35] Pope Francis, Apostolic Constitution *Praedicate Evangelium*, March 19, 2022 (hereafter, PE), https://www.vatican.va/content/francesco/en/apost_constitutions/documents/20220319-costituzione-ap-praedicate-evangelium

Christian centuries. Over time, however, the consecration of virgins was restricted to nuns. On March 25, 1927, the Congregation for Religious responded negatively to a request for the possibility of granting the consecration of virgins to women living in the world.[36] This was only made possible by the liturgical reform after the Second Vatican Council. The revised *Ordo Consecrationis Virginum* of 1970 provides for the consecration to a life of virginity not only for nuns but also for women[37] living in the world.[38] The ordinary minister of the consecration of virgins is the diocesan bishop, who may delegate this function to an auxiliary bishop or to a priest (see c. 1169 §1).[39] Nuns who are consecrated virgins remain under the authority of their superior. Canon 604 concerns consecrated virgins who do not belong to a religious institute and live in the world.

The prerequisites for receiving the consecration of virgins for women living in the world are that

a) they have never married or lived in public or open violation of chastity;
b) by their age, prudence, and universally approved character, they give assurance of perseverance in a life of chastity dedicated to the service of the church and of their neighbor; and
c) they be admitted to this consecration by the bishop who is the ordinary of the place.[40]

.html: "The eremitical life and the *ordo virginum* . . . are forms of consecrated life" (126 §1).

[36] In *AAS* 19 (1927): 138–39.

[37] The *ordo virginum* is restricted to women.

[38] This is the approved liturgical rite referred to in c. 604 §1. For further details, see Nichola Emsley, "The Rite of Consecration of Virgins," in *Handbook for Liturgical Studies*, vol. IV: *Sacraments and Sacramentals*, ed. Anscar J. Chupungco (Liturgical Press, 2000), 331–42.

[39] This was confirmed by the Prefect of the Congregation for Divine Worship in a letter of February 22, 1986, Prot.-N. 286/86.

[40] See *Ordo Consecrationis Virginum*, 5.

It is for the bishop to decide on the conditions under which women living in the world are to undertake a life of perpetual virginity.

On June 8, 2018, the Congregation for Institutes of Consecrated Life and Societies of Apostolic Life published the instruction *Ecclesiae Sponsae Imago* on the *ordo virginum*.[41] It states that vocational discernment, formation before consecration, and ongoing formation after consecration are the responsibility not only of the candidate or consecrated virgin, but also of the diocesan bishop, who may appoint a delegate or establish a service or team for vocational discernment and formation, depending on the number of consecrated virgins in his diocese. The preparatory period should be divided into three phases: formation, evaluation, and final discernment (see ESI 81). Determining the manner in which the programs of formation are to be carried out is the responsibility of the diocesan bishop. The minimum age for admission to the preparation period is eighteen, while for celebration of the consecration it is twenty-five (see ESI 82). Physical virginity is not necessarily required.[42] Upon completion of the period of formation, the candidate may apply in writing for admission. Together with the request, a recommendation of the spiritual accompanier must be submitted (see ESI 104). The definitive discernment is the responsibility of the diocesan bishop (see ESI 104–106). A register of the *ordo virginum* is to be kept in

[41] CICLSAL, *Ecclesiae Sponsae Imago*: Instruction on the *Ordo Virginum* (Libreria Editrice Vaticana, 2018), also available at https://press.vatican.va/content/salastampa/en/bollettino/pubblico/2018/07/04/180704d.html (hereafter, ESI).

[42] "In this context it should be kept in mind that the call to give witness to the Church's virginal, spousal and fruitful love for Christ is not reducible to the symbol of physical integrity. Thus to have kept her body in perfect continence or to have practiced the virtue of chastity in an exemplary way, while of great importance with regard to the discernment, are not essential prerequisites in the absence of which admittance to consecration is not possible" (ESI 88).

each diocese to document the consecrations that have taken place. A consecration should also be annotated in the baptismal register (see ESI 107). The consecrated virgin receives a certificate of her consecration.[43]

Consecrated virgins, according to c. 604, are women living in the world. They are not entitled to support from the diocesan bishop but must provide for their own subsistence and social security. Although it is desirable that a consecrated virgin be integrated into the life of her parish and her diocese, there is no obligation to volunteer. Consecrated virgins may form associations for mutual support (see c. 604 §2). The establishment of such associations is the responsibility of the diocesan bishop at the diocesan level and of the bishops' conference at the national level[44] (see c. 604 §3). At the international level, it is the task of the Dicastery for Institutes of Consecrated Life and Societies of Apostolic Life to establish such associations (see PE 126 §2). Membership in an association is the free choice of each consecrated virgin and is not obligatory. Leaving an association does not mean leaving the state of consecrated virgin (see ESI 65). Likewise, consecrated virgins are free to live in a common household in order to help each other and lead a common spiritual life (see ESI 65).

A transfer of a consecrated virgin to another diocese requires the consent of both bishops involved (see ESI 62). After having received consecration, there may be various reasons that lead to a separation from the *ordo virginum*. Universal law is silent on this matter. Further details of the procedure are given in the instruction *Ecclesiae Sponsae Imago* (see ESI 69–73). If a consecrated virgin wishes to enter an institute of

[43] A template can be found in Amy Hereford, *See I Am Making Something New: A Canonical and Pastoral Guidebook on New Institutes, Diocesan Hermits and Consecrated Virgins and New Forms of Consecrated Life* (CreateSpace, 2018), 135.

[44] In the United States, for example, there is the United States Association of Consecrated Virgins.

consecrated life or society of apostolic life, she should address a written request to the diocesan bishop, together with a letter from the superior of the institute or society concerning existing contacts. The bishop forwards the request, together with his own opinion, to the Apostolic See, which will decide on the matter and issue arrangements for each particular case. If, for very grave reasons, a consecrated virgin wishes to leave the *ordo virginum*, she should address a written request for dispensation to the diocesan bishop, who may grant the dispensation after an in-depth scrutiny of the reasons for her request. Not least, there may be reasons for dismissal from the *ordo virginum*. By analogous application of c. 694, a consecrated virgin is ipso facto dismissed if she has notoriously defected from the Catholic faith or has married, even only civilly. In this case, the bishop collects the evidence and declares her dismissal. By analogous application of c. 695 §1, if a consecrated virgin is accused of very serious external and imputable crimes, the diocesan bishop is to begin the process of dismissal. He first informs the consecrated virgin of the accusations and of the evidence, giving her the opportunity to defend herself. If the bishop deems the defense to be insufficient, he issues the decree of dismissal, which must, at least in summary, state the reasons for dismissal and, in order to be valid, indicate the right to recourse within ten days of notification. The decree shall be sent to the Apostolic See, together with all the documents, for confirmation. The decree takes effect upon notification. A recourse has a suspensive effect. In all cases, the separation from the *ordo virginum* must be recorded in the register of the *ordo virginum* and in the baptismal register.

Further reading: Nancy Bauer, "'Ecclesiae sponsae imago': Instruction on the Order of Consecrated Virgins Aids in Implementing Canon 604 and the Rite of Consecration," *Jur* 77 (2021): 73–101; Congregation for Institutes of Consecrated

Life and Societies of Apostolic Life, *Ecclesiae Sponsae Imago: Instruction on the Ordo Virginum* (Libreria Editrice Vaticana, 2021); Nichola Emsley, "The Rite of Consecration of Virgins," in *Handbook for Liturgical Studies*, vol. IV: *Sacraments and Sacramentals*, ed. Anscar J. Chupungco (Liturgical Press, 2000), 331–42.

c) Consecrated Widows

In apostolic times, there was an *ordo viduarum* (see esp. 1 Tim 5:3-16). This venerable institution fell into oblivion over time. It was not until the middle of the twentieth century that attempts were made to revive the *ordo viduarum*, first in France. The Code of Canon Law is silent on the consecration of widows. The Code of Canons of the Eastern Churches on the other hand recognizes the order of widows (see c. 570 CCEO). *Vita Consecrata* 7 mentions consecrated widows,[45] who "through a vow of perpetual chastity as a sign of the Kingdom of God, consecrate their state of life in order to devote themselves to prayer and the service of the Church." In the absence of regulations in universal law, it is left to the discretion of the diocesan bishop to decide whether and under what conditions consecration of widows is practiced in his diocese. Since at this writing there is no *editio typica* for the Latin Catholic Church for the rite of consecration of widows, it is up to the diocesan bishop to approve such a rite for his territory (see c. 838 §4).

Further reading: Christina Hip-Flores, "Consecrated Widows: Altars of God: A Restored Ancient Vocation in the Catholic Church," *Logos: A Journal of Catholic Thought and Culture* 22 (2019): 108–30.

[45] Besides the consecration of widows, *Vita Consecrata* 7 also mentions the consecration of widowers. In the early church, however, the *ordo viduarum* was reserved for widowed women.

d) New Forms of Consecrated Life (c. 605)

From the nineteenth century, congregations with simple vows and, from the twentieth century, secular institutes took their place alongside the religious orders. The Code recognizes diocesan hermits and consecrated virgins as other forms of consecrated life. Canon law is also open to new forms of consecrated life (see c. 605; VC 62). The diocesan bishops are called to discern new gifts of consecrated life and to assist to promote them. The approval of new forms of consecrated life, however, is reserved only to the Apostolic See.

New forms of consecrated life are those that do not fit into the scheme prescribed by canon law. The basic requirement for classification as consecrated life is a commitment to the evangelical counsels. Whether the commitment must always include all three evangelical counsels, or can be limited to one or two, is controversial.

Further reading: Maria Casey, "The Evolution of New Forms of Consecrated Life," *StudCan* 36 (2002): 463–86; Joseph A. Galante, "Consecrated Life: New Forms and New Institutes," *CLSA Proceedings* 48 (1986): 118–25; Przemysław Michowicz, "Legal Difficulties and/or Impossibility Concerning New Forms of Consecrated Life (c. 605)," *StudCan* 48 (2014): 171–88.

17. Equal Applicability of the Law (c. 606)

What is established in the Code for institutes of consecrated life and their members applies equally to both sexes, unless the context of the norm or the nature of the matter indicates otherwise (see c. 606). A significant difference is that the major superiors of institutes of women are not ordinaries, since that function can be held only by clerics. Nuns occupy a special position among women religious, since they are more dependent on the Apostolic See because of various special regulations. However, what is intended to protect nunneries and their members can also be seen as a violation of due autonomy and the principle of subsidiarity. The instruction *Cor Orans* is judged differently when it comes to the equality of male and female religious. On the one hand, it limited the powers of the diocesan bishop and thus gave more autonomy to the monasteries and the federation to which they belong. On the other hand, the formation period for nuns has been significantly extended in comparison to that of male and female religious who are not nuns, which has been criticized as an unjustified inequality.

Chapter Two

Religious Institutes (cc. 607–709)

Members of religious institutes commit themselves by public vows to the evangelical counsels and lead a common life as brothers or sisters (see c. 607 §2). They have in common with the members of secular institutes the commitment to the evangelical counsels. The difference between religious institutes and secular institutes is that members of religious institutes lead a common life.

1. **Religious Houses and Their Erection and Suppression** (cc. 608–616)

The obligation to common life requires a religious house in which common life takes place. For this reason, a religious community must live under the authority of a lawfully appointed superior in a house that has been lawfully erected. Each house must have at least an oratory where the Eucharist is celebrated[1] and reserved (see c. 608). An oratory is "a place for divine worship designated by permission of the ordinary for the benefit of some community or group of the faithful who gather in it and to which other members of the faithful can also come with the consent of the competent superior"

[1] At least twice a month, as far as possible, according to c. 934 §2.

(c. 1223). Instead of a chapel or in addition to it, a religious house may have a church with the permission of the diocesan bishop (see c. 1215 §3). A church is "a sacred building designated for divine worship to which the faithful have the right of entry for the exercise, especially the public exercise, of divine worship" (c. 1214). Whether a religious house should have an oratory or a church depends on whether the house of worship is used primarily for the community's internal worship or whether the community offers public worship and other services of pastoral care.

The erection of a religious house is the responsibility of the competent authority in accordance with the constitutions, with the prior written consent of the diocesan bishop (see c. 609 §1). The erection of a monastery of nuns also requires the permission of the Apostolic See (see c. 609 §2). The specific requirements for the erection of a religious house should be set forth in the institute's proper law, since the requirements may vary greatly according to the nature of the institute. For example, the requirements for a charterhouse are quite different from those for a Jesuit community. As general minimum requirements for the erection of a religious house, universal law states that there must be a benefit to the church and to the institute, with appropriate safeguards for those things which are necessary for the proper conduct of the religious life of the members in accordance with the proper purposes and spirit of the institute (see c. 610). The consent of the diocesan bishop to erect a religious house implies the right to live in conformity with the patrimony of the institute, to carry out the functions proper to the institute, and for clerical institutes to have a church—which, according to c. 1215 §3, requires the special permission of the diocesan bishop—and to perform sacred ministries (see c. 611). With regard to the exercise of apostolic works, the relevant norms are to be observed, in particular that the diocesan bishop is responsible for the direction and the coordination of all apostolic works and activities in his diocese (see c. 680). If a religious house intends to undertake apostolic works other than those for which it was founded, the consent of the diocesan bishop is required, except when the change concerns only internal government and discipline[2] (see c. 612).

Unless the constitutions provide otherwise, a religious house of canons regular or of monks under the governance and care of its own moderator is autonomous (see c. 613). Constitutions usually provide for a gradual path to independent status, beginning with the erection of a dependent house, which is raised to the status of an independent house by the competent authority of the institute when the conditions mentioned in the constitutions are met. An autonomous house is a public juridic person according to the norms of universal law (see c. 116). The moderator of an autonomous house and his vicar are by law major superiors (see cc. 613, 620).

Monasteries of nuns may be associated with an institute of men. This is the case, for example, with Cistercian, Trappist, and Carthusian nuns. In the case of Benedictine nuns, it depends on the congregation. Associated monasteries maintain their own way of life and governance according to their constitutions. Mutual rights and obligations are to be defined in the proper law and other documents. An association is more than a spiritual aggregation according to c. 580. Spiritual good is to be derived from association, such as the enhancement of the common patrimony. Proper law may, but does not necessarily have to, establish that the supreme moderator of the institute of men also has authority over the monasteries of nuns.

If an autonomous monastery is not part of an institute and is not associated to another institute so that above the local superior there is no other superior who possesses true power

[2] For example, a house built as a novitiate and then converted into a retirement home for elderly members of the institute.

over the monastery (e.g., abbot president or abbot general),[3] the monastery is entrusted to the special vigilance of the diocesan bishop (see c. 615). In practice, this mainly concerns monasteries of nuns that are not associated with an institute of men according to c. 614. The competence of the diocesan bishop in this case includes:[4]

- presiding at the elections of a superior (see c. 625 §2);
- the right and duty to carry out the canonical visit (see c. 628 §2,1°), accompanied by the president of the federation as co-visitor in the case of a monastery of nuns (see CO 111);
- examining the annual report of the administration of temporal goods of the monastery (see c. 637);
- giving written consent for certain financial transactions, required for validity (see c. 638 §4), for autonomous monasteries of nuns only if established by its proper law[5]; and
- confirming an indult of departure of a nun in temporary vows to be valid (see c. 688 §2).[6]

The supreme moderator, after consulting the diocesan bishop, may suppress a religious house lawfully erected according to the norms of the constitutions (see c. 616 §1). The

[3] The president of a federation of monasteries of nuns is not a major superior and does not possess true power over the monasteries of the federation (see CO 110).

[4] Regarding autonomous monasteries of nuns, see CO 81.

[5] See CO 81d. Otherwise, the written permission of the major superior is required with the consent of the council or the conventual chapter, and the opinion of the president of the federation (see CO 52). This derogation from c. 638 §4 was approved by the pope *in forma specifica*.

[6] To decide on a dismissal now belongs to the major superior with the consent of the council according to the apostolic letter *Competentias Quasdam*.

consent of the diocesan bishop is not required. The proper law of an institute is to make provisions for the use of the temporal goods of a suppressed house, without prejudice to the intentions of the founders or donors, or to the rights that have been legitimately acquired. For the following cases, universal law provides special rules for suppression:

- The suppression of the only house of an institute belongs to the Apostolic See, which also decides on temporal goods in this case (see c. 616 §2). This norm corresponds to the norm that the suppression of an institute is reserved to the Apostolic See (see c. 584).
- The suppression of an autonomous house referred to in c. 613 belongs to the general chapter, unless the constitutions provide otherwise (see c. 616 §3).
- The suppression of an autonomous monastery of nuns belongs to the Apostolic See, with due regard for the provisions of the constitutions concerning its temporal goods (see c. 616 §4). If the constitutions do not provide for the use of the temporal goods in the event of suppression, they go to the juridic person immediately superior (see c. 123).

Further reading: Anne Bamberg, "Monasterio autónomo y vigilancia particular del Obispo diocesano: En torno a la interpretación del c. 615 del Código de Derecho Canónico," *IC* 48 (2008): 477–92; Sharon Holland, "Religious House According to Canon 608," *Jur* 50 (1990): 524–52.

2. The Governance of Institutes (cc. 617–640)

The governance of an institute is exercised by persons and bodies. Bodies are in particular councils and chapters. Superiors and chapters have the authority over the members as defined by universal law and the constitutions (see c. 596 §1).

a) Superiors and Their Councils (cc. 617–630)

Superiors are to carry out their function and to exercise their power in accordance with the norms of universal law and proper law (see c. 617). They are to have their own council, the assistance of which they are to use in the exercise of their office (see c. 627).

aa) Authority of Superiors (cc. 618–619)

Superiors are more than mere ecclesiastical functionaries. Rather, their ministry has both a juridical and a spiritual dimension. Superiors are to exercise their office in a spirit of service (see c. 618). They are to be devoted to the will of God and to govern their subordinates as children of God, with respect for the human person. Mutual obedience is essential because it promotes unity and contributes to the good of the institute and the church. Superiors should listen to their subordinates and encourage their voluntary obedience. However, this does not limit the authority of the superior to decide and prescribe what is to be done within the scope of his competence: "In community life which is inspired by the Holy Spirit, each individual engages in a fruitful dialogue with the others in order to discover the Father's will. At the same time, together they recognize in the one who presides an expression of the fatherhood of God and the exercise of authority received from God, at the service of discernment and communion" (VC 92).

This understanding of the authority of superiors can be characterized as a common search for the best solution and reflects the understanding of synodal governance in religious institutes. A process of discernment involves the whole community. The final decision rests with the superior within the limits of his authority, who is also responsible for the implementation of the decisions made: "*Community discernment* is a rather useful process, even if not easy or automatic, for involving human competence, spiritual wisdom and personal detachment. Where it is practised with faith and seriousness, it can provide superiors with optimal conditions for making necessary decisions in the best interests of fraternal life and of mission. When a decision has been made in accordance with the procedures established by proper law, superiors need perseverance and strength to ensure that what has been decided not remain mere words on paper."[7]

A paternalistic style of governance is therefore excluded. In addition to the principle of mutual obedience, the law also prescribes organs of participation or consultation (see c. 633). However, a collegial structure of governance in such a way that a superior becomes a mere executor of community decisions is also precluded.[8]

Further reading: Congregation for Institutes of Consecrated Life and Societies of Apostolic Life, *The Service of Authority and Obedience: Faciem Tuam, Domine, Requiram*, https://www.vatican.va/roman_curia/congregations/ccscrlife/documents/rc_con_ccscrlife_doc_20080511_autorita-obbedienza_en.html.

bb) Types of Superiors (cc. 620–622)

There are three types of superiors:

- local superior (*superior localis*)
- major superior (*superior maior*)
- supreme moderator (*supremus moderator*)

[7] CICLSAL, *Fraternal Life in Community: "Congregavit Nos in Unum Christi Amor,"* February 2, 1994, no. 50c, https://www.vatican.va/roman_curia/congregations/ccscrlife/documents/rc_con_ccscrlife_doc_02021994_fraternal-life-in-community_en.html.

[8] Cf. Congregation for Religious and Secular Institutes, *Decretum* of February 2, 1972, *AAS* 64 (1972): 393–94: "*D. An . . . regimen collegiale ordinarium et exclusivum admitti fas sit, sive pro toto Institute religioso, sive pro provincia, sive pro singulis domibus, ita ut Superior, si habetur, sit merus executor? R. Negative.*"

The superior of a religious house as well as their vicar are local superiors. The superior of an entire institute, a province,[9] or an autonomous house as well as their vicar are major superiors. The abbot primate and the superior of a monastic congregation are also major superiors, but because of the federal structure of monastic congregations, they do not have all the power that universal law grants to major superiors but only the power that proper law grants to them. A major superior who has authority over all the provinces, houses, and members of an institute is called the supreme moderator (see c. 622). Major superiors of clerical institutes of pontifical right are ordinaries for their own members (see c. 134 §1). Except for territorial abbots, they are not local ordinaries (see c. 134 §2). In religious institutes, along with the various competencies in penal law, it is, in particular, up to ordinaries to:

- confer the ministries of lector and acolyte (see Pope Paul VI, Apostolic Letter *Ministeria quaedam* 9),
- dispense from irregularities and impediments not reserved to the Apostolic See (see c. 1047 §4),
- give written permission for the repair of precious images (see c. 1189),
- bless sacred places except for churches (see c. 1207),
- issue a decree that permanently turns over sacred places to profane use (see c. 1212), and

[9] A province is a "grouping of several houses which constitutes an immediate part of the same institute under the same superior and has been canonically erected by legitimate authority" (c. 621). A province can be constituted only with at least three houses (see c. 115 §2), but this minimum number is no longer required for its continued existence after it has been legally erected. Institutes sometimes provide in their proper law for pro-provinces with fewer than three houses.

- grant permission to establish an oratory (see c. 1224 §1).[10]

cc) Election and Designation of Superiors (cc. 623–626)

The supreme moderator of an institute is to be chosen by canonical election in accordance with the norm of the constitutions (see c. 625).[11] The right of election rests with the general chapter (see c. 631 §1). The election of the supreme moderator of an institute of diocesan right is presided over by the bishop of the principal seat (see c. 625 §2). All other superiors are either elected or appointed according to the provisions of the constitutions (see c. 625 §3). If superiors are elected, they need to be confirmed by the competent major superior. If superiors are appointed, the appointment must be preceded by an appropriate consultation. This is an obligation to obtain counsel according to c. 127 § 2,2°, which means that an appointment is invalid if the prior consultation has not taken place. In the conferring of offices (see c. 146–163) and in elections (see c. 164–179), the provisions of universal law and of proper law are to be observed. Any abuse is to be prevented. The person appointed by the superior or elected by those entitled to vote should be one whom they consider truly worthy and suitable in the sight of God and for the good of the institute, without regard to person. The direct or indirect procurement of votes for oneself or for others is not permitted (c. 626). Superiors of clerical institutes are obliged, according to the provisions of the constitutions, to make in person a

[10] For further details, see Giorgio Giovanelli, "The Investigatio Praevia and the Role of the Ordinary for Criminal Procedures," *The Canonist* 13 (2022): 217–27.

[11] Regarding the possibility of a direct election of the supreme moderator, see Ellen O'Hara, "Is It Permissible to Have Direct Election (Non-chapter) of Supreme Moderators and Major Superiors?," in *Selected Issues in Religious Law*, ed. Patrick J. Cogan (CLSA, 1997), 15–16.

profession of faith according to the formula approved by the Apostolic See (see c. 833, 8°) and to take an oath of fidelity.[12]

The requirements for the election and appointment of superiors are largely to be determined in the proper law. Consequently, universal law affords the individual institutes the leeway to establish their own criteria according to their patrimony. Universal law merely stipulates that a reasonable period of time must have elapsed after perpetual or definitive profession before someone can be elected or appointed as a superior (see c. 623). This period is to be determined in the proper law or, in the case of major superiors, in the constitutions.

The term of office of a superior is to be determined by proper law. Universal law merely prescribes that the election or appointment should be for a certain and appropriate period of time, according to nature and needs of the institute, and that care should be taken to ensure that superiors who are elected or appointed for a definite period do not remain in office for too long without interruption (see c. 624 §§1–2). Some religious institutes have the tradition of electing superiors for life. For instance, abbots of Benedictine monasteries were traditionally elected for life, and the superior general of the Society of Jesus is still elected for life. In order to take these traditions into account, the constitutions can determine something other than a definite and limited term of office for the supreme moderator and for superiors of an autonomous house (see c. 624 §1), thus allowing, for example, Benedictine abbots to be elected either for life or for an indefinite period of time until they reach a certain age limit.

[12] See Congregation for the Doctrine of the Faith, "Profession of Faith," https://www.vatican.va/roman_curia/congregations/cfaith/documents/rc_con_cfaith_doc_1998_professio-fidei_en.html; Latin orig. at Congregatio pro doctrina fidei, "Professio fidei et iusiurandum fidelitatis in suscipiendo officio nomine Ecclesiae exercendo una cum nota doctrinali adnexa," June 29, 1998, *AAS* 90 (1998): 542–51.

The norms concerning the loss of office are laid down in cc. 184–196. An ecclesiastical office can be lost by the lapse of a predetermined time, reaching the age determined by law, resignation, transfer, removal, or privation (see c. 184 §1). If a superior is elected for a limited period of time, he loses his office upon the expiration of the period for which he was elected. The same applies if an age limit is established by law. In both instances, the loss of office only becomes effective at the time of its written communication by the competent authority (see c. 186). A superior may resign from his office for a just cause (see c. 187). The resignation must be made to the competent authority according to proper law (see c. 189 §1). If the resignation requires acceptance by the competent authority, this authority may only accept it if it is based on a just and proportionate reason (see c. 189 §2). Furthermore, superiors may be transferred to another office or removed from their office for reasons set forth in the proper law (see c. 624 §3). A superior can be removed from office by decree of the competent authority or by the law itself (see c. 192). A superior is removed from his office by law itself in the event of loss of the clerical state, public defection from the Catholic faith or from the communion of the church, or marriage or attempted marriage in the case of a cleric (see c. 194). In the two latter cases, removal from office can be enforced only if it is established by a declaration of a competent authority. These two cases also entail a dismissal from the institute ipso facto (see c. 694 §1,1–2°). In certain cases, the deprivation of an office may be imposed as a penalty (see c. 1336 §4,1°). Upon a superior who loses his office by reason of age or resignation that has been accepted, the title of *emeritus* can be conferred by the competent authority (see c. 185). The proper law of an institute may provide that this honorary title is conferred by the law itself. In addition, other situations than those mentioned in universal law for conferring the title of *eremitus* may be established.

Further reading: Rosemary Smith, "Election of Major Superiors," in *Selected Issues in Religious Law*, ed. Patrick J. Cogan (Canon Law Society of America, 1997), 17–25.

dd) Obligations of Superiors (cc. 628–630)

One of the essential obligations of a superior is to visit the houses and members under his jurisdiction according to the provisions of proper law (see c. 628 §1). The competent superior and the frequency of visitations are to be determined by proper law. The visitation of the individual houses of an institute of diocesan right located in his territory, as well as the visitation of autonomous monasteries mentioned in c. 615,[13] are the responsibility of the diocesan bishop.

Superiors have the obligation to reside in their own house (see c. 629). The purpose of this provision is to ensure that superiors fulfill their obligations. Depending on the nature of an institute, the regulations may vary. In monastic communities, for example, they differ from those of apostolic communities. For this reason, further details, especially the exceptions, are to be regulated by the proper law. A superior who gravely violates the obligation of residence is to be punished with a just penalty, not excluding deprivation of ministry after a warning (see c. 1396).

Another obligation of superiors, which is essential not least for the prevention of spiritual abuse, is to allow the members due freedom with regard to the sacrament of penance and the direction of conscience (see c. 630 §1). All religious are free to choose their confessor and spiritual director. The discipline of the institute, however, is to be observed. This includes, for example, the obligation of enclosure, especially in monasteries of nuns. Furthermore, confession and direction of conscience must not be used as a pretext for avoiding common prayer or

[13] In the case of an autonomous monastery of nuns, the diocesan bishop is accompanied by the president of the federation to which the monastery belongs as co-visitor (see CO 111).

assigned work. In accordance with the norms of the proper law of the institute, superiors are to ensure the availability of suitable confessors to whom religious can frequently confess (see c. 630 §2). There is no obligation on the part of the religious to receive the sacrament of penance from them. They may also turn to other confessors, provided that the discipline of the institute is observed. In monasteries of nuns, houses of formation, and more numerous lay communities, the superior, after consultation with the community, should see to it that ordinary confessors approved by the local ordinary are available, although there is no obligation to receive the sacrament of penance from them (see c. 630 §3). In order not to confuse *forum externum* and *forum internum*, superiors are not allowed to hear confessions of their subjects unless they request it on their own initiative (see c. 630 §4). The same applies to the director of novices and his associates with regard to the confessions of novices (see c. 985). Since superiors exercise authority over their subjects, a conflict could arise because superiors may not use knowledge acquired in confession in the exercise of their authority (see c. 984 §2). For this reason, superiors are well advised not to hear the confessions of their subjects, even if they ask them to do so, and this is a legitimate reason for a superior to refuse to hear confession of a subject (see c. 843 §1). On the one hand, superiors are forbidden to demand, directly or indirectly, that their subjects manifest their conscience to them.[14] On the other hand, religious should approach their superiors in trust and to open their consciences freely and voluntarily (see c. 630 §5). This way, superiors are better able to fulfill the spiritual dimension of their ministry and to be a spiritual director for their subjects.

[14] The Society of Jesus has the custom established in its constitutions that all professed members manifest their conscience to their superior once a year. The obligation to do so in the sacrament of confession was abolished at the 34th General Congregation in 1995. See José Luis Sánchez-Girón Renedo, "Sentido y finalidad de un privilegio relativo al c. 630," *Estudios Eclesiásticos* 81 (2006): 725–60.

It must be clear that the manifestation of conscience to a superior must be completely voluntary and without any coercion. The question arises, however, whether it is necessary for a superior to be the spiritual director of his subjects. In practice, it is advisable not to entrust spiritual direction to the superiors, not only to prevent spiritual abuse but also for the practical reason of maintaining an external perspective in spiritual direction.

Further reading: Rose McDermott, "The Service of Authority and Obedience: The Canonical Visitation of Major Superiors (Canon 628 §§1,3)," *StudCan* 99 (2010): 527–55.

ee) Councils (c. 627)

All superiors are to have a council to assist them in the exercise of their office according to the provisions of the constitutions (see c. 627 §1). Councils are thus to be established at all levels of an institute: the entire institute, provinces, and individual houses. The members of a council have different titles in different institutes, such as assistants, consultors, councilors, deans, or seniors. Only for the council of the supreme moderator does the Code of Canon Law stipulate that it must consist of at least four members in order for the decision to issue a decree of dismissal to be valid (see c. 699 §1). Otherwise, universal law does not specify the number of councilors, leaving it to the proper law. In practice, the number of councilors usually depends on the size of the institute, province, or house, but it should be at least two. The manner in which the members of the council are appointed is also left to proper law. Usually, certain persons are ex officio members of the council. The other members of the council are elected in some institutes and appointed by the superior in others. The term of office of the councilors is also determined by proper law, with some institutions linking their term of office to the term of office of the superior. Council members are obliged to give their opinions sincerely and to maintain confidentiality, especially in important matters (see c. 127 §3).

Chapters are responsible for dealing with extraordinary matters, while the superior and his council conduct the day-to-day business. The participation of the council can be in the form of a consultative vote (*votum consultivum*) or a deliberative vote (*votum deliberativum*). That is, the superior must either first consult his council and then decide themself, or they need the approval of his council in order to act. The council must be convoked in accordance with the provisions of c. 166 (see c. 127 §1). Only in the case of a consultative vote, proper law can provide that the council members need not meet in person but may be consulted individually by letter, fax, email, telephone, or videoconference. In the case of a deliberative vote, personal attendance is generally required, and voting by letter or proxy is generally excluded, unless otherwise provided by proper law (see c. 167 §1). In the course of the COVID-19 pandemic, Pope Francis granted the Congregation for Institutes of Consecrated Life and Societies of Apostolic Life an extraordinary faculty to derogate in individual cases from the obligation of the councilors to be physically present according to the provision of c. 166 §1 and to allow digital meetings of councils.[15] This was not intended to be a permanent solution but was introduced as an extraordinary possibility for the duration of the pandemic. After the pandemic was overcome, the Dicastery for Institutes of Consecrated Life and Societies of Apostolic Life issued a circular letter on March 19, 2023,[16] stating that a dispensation from

[15] See CICLSAL, "Circular Letter to General Moderators," July 1, 2020, Prot. N. Sp.R. 2452/20. *RRAO* 2020: 13–15.

[16] See Dicastery for Institutes of Consecrated Life and Societies of Apostolic Life (hereafter, DICLSAL), "Circular Letter on the Utilization of Computer-Telematic Tools for Acts of Governance Referred to in Canons 627, 127 and 166," March 19, 2023, Prot. N. Sp.R. 2452/20. *RRAO* 2023: 46–47.

the Apostolic See is no longer required to hold online council meetings. However, it states that online meetings are an extraordinary form and must not become an ordinary solution.[17] The dicastery explicitly excludes certain matters from discussion in online council meetings: *delicta graviora*, separation from the institute, admission to perpetual profession, admission to sacred orders, provisions regarding the public exercise of sacred orders and sacred ministry, and acts of extraordinary administration.[18] Institutes should include detailed provisions regarding online council meetings in their proper law.

The cases in which a superior must obtain consent or counsel are determined in universal law and proper law (see c. 127 §2).

In the following cases, the superior must obtain a vote from their council. If it is a consultative vote or a deliberative vote is to be determined in proper law:

- admission to temporary profession (c. 656,3°)
- admission to perpetual profession (c. 658)

In addition to the cases mentioned in proper law, universal law prescribes that the superior must obtain a consultative vote from their council in the following cases:

- exclusion from further profession (c. 689 § 1)
- initiation of the process of dismissal in cases of facultative dismissal (c. 697)

In addition to the cases mentioned in proper law, universal law prescribes that the superior must obtain a deliberative vote from his council in the following cases:

[17] See DICLSAL, "Circular Letter on the Utilization of Computer-Telematic Tools," no. 1.

[18] See DICLSAL, "Circular Letter on the Utilization of Computer-Telematic Tools," no. 2.

- alienation of temporal goods and any other affair in which the patrimonial condition of a juridic person can worsen (c. 638 §3)
- erection, transfer, and suppression of a novitiate house (c. 647 §1)
- permission that a candidate can make the novitiate in another house of the institute (c. 647 §2)
- lengthy absence from the house (c. 665 §1)
- transfer to another institute (c. 684 §1)
- departure from an institute (c. 686 §§1.3)
- indult of departure during the time of temporary profession (c. 688 §2)
- readmission without repeating the novitiate after completing the novitiate or after profession (c. 690)
- statement of the case of a dismissal ipso facto from an institute (c. 694 §2)
- collegial decision on a dismissal from the institute (c. 699 §1)
- expulsion from a house by the local superior (c. 703)

If a consultative vote is required, an act of a superior is invalid if they have not heard their councilors. After having heard their councilors, the decision rests with the superior. Though they are not obliged to accept the opinion of their councilors, a superior should not act contrary to the opinion of their council, especially if it is unanimous, without a serious reason (see c. 127 §2,2°). If a deliberative vote is required, an act of a superior is invalid if they have not sought the consent of their council or if they act despite a negative vote of their council (see c. 127 §2,1°). For a vote to be valid, at least an absolute majority of those who are to be convoked must be present (see c. 119,2°), unless proper law provides otherwise. If a person has the right to vote in their own name under several titles, they may vote only once (see c. 168). However, if proper law provides for voting by proxy, a person can have one vote in their own name and additional votes as a proxy, while proper law may limit the number of votes as a proxy. Whether a vote is secret or not is to be determined by proper law. Unless proper law provides otherwise, an absolute majority of the votes of those present is required, abstentions and invalid votes being counted (see c. 119,2°). A superior cannot participate in the vote of their council or break a tie.[19] The collegial governance of an institute, province, or house by a superior with their council or by a council alone is not possible.[20] It is possible, however, for the proper law to indicate specific cases in which the superior acts collegially with their council.

[19] See Pontifical Commission for Authentic Interpretation of the Code of Canon Law, "Authentic Interpretation," May 14, 1985, *AAS* 77 (1985): 771: "*D. Utrum cum iure statuatur ad actus ponendos Superiorem indigere consensu alicuius Collegii vel personarum coetus, ad normam can. 127, § 1, ipse Superior ius habeat ferendi suffragium cum aliis, saltem ad paritatem suffragiorum dirimendam. R. Negative.*" In practice, the DICLSAL, when approving constitutions, leaves it up to each institute to decide whether to grant the superior the right to vote together with their council. The dicastery assumes a doubt about the law as to whether the authentic interpretation also applies to religious institutes, since c. 627 refers to the proper law of an institute. For further details, see Bruno Esposito, "La partecipazione del superiore religioso alle votazioni con il suo consiglio quando il diritto richiede il consenso: Questione risolta? Alcune riflessioni sui cann. 127 § 1 e 627," *PRC* 95 (2006): 37–68; Alberto Perlasca, "L'interpretazione autentica delle leggi ecclesiali: Il superiore e il suo consiglio (can. 127 § 1)," *QDE* 23 (2010): 311–23.

[20] See Congregation for the Religious and the Secular Institutes, "Decretum circa regiminis ordinarii rationem," February 2, 1972, *AAS* 64 (1972): 393–94: "*D. An . . . regimen collegiale ordinarium et exclusivum admitti fas sit, sive pro toto Institute religioso, sive pro provincia, sive pro singulis domibus, ita ut Superior, si habetur, sit merus executor? R. Negative.*"

Further reading: Maurizi Costa, "Il governo del superiore e il suo consiglio: Dati canonici e rilettura spirituale," *PRC* 93 (2004): 189–221; Dicastery for Institutes of Consecrated Life and Societies of Apostolic Life, "Circular Letter on the Utilization of Computer-Telematic Tools for Acts of Governance Referred to in Canons 627, 127 and 166," March 19, 2023, Prot. N. Sp.R. 2452/20, *RRAO* 2023: 46–47; Bruno Esposito, "La partecipazione del superiore religioso alle votazioni con il suo consiglio quando il diritto richiede il consenso: Questione risolta? Alcune riflessioni sui cann. 127 §1 e 627," *PRC* 95 (2006): 37–68; Priamo Etzi, "Il consiglio del superiore religioso: Normativa e dibattiti (cann. 627 e 127)," VC 39 (2003): 612–35; Rose McDermott, "The Role of Councils in Religious Institutes," *Studies in Church Law* 5 (2009): 201–24; James H. Provost, "Manner of Superior Seeking Council's Consent," *RRAO* 1995: 38–39; Alfredo Rava, "Il governo degli istituti di vita consacrata in tempo di Covid-19," *QDE* 36 (2023): 448–63; Silvia Recchi, "Strutture di partecipazione negli Istituti di vita consacrata," *QDE* 1 (1988): 52–59.

b) Chapters (cc. 631–633)

Chapters as participatory or consultative bodies have a long tradition in religious life. The name comes from the Benedictine monastic tradition of meeting daily to listen to the reading of a chapter from the Rule of St. Benedict. During these meetings, questions about monastic life were also discussed. The Cistercian order, founded in 1098, had a general chapter as its supreme authority from the beginning. At the Fourth Lateran Council (1215), all monasteries were required to form associations and hold regular chapters based on the Cistercian model. However, it was not until the Council of Trent (1545–63) that this obligation was actually implemented.[21]

[21] See David Knowles, *Christian Monasticism* (Weidenfeld & Nicolson, 1969), 112–23.

The general chapter is the supreme authority in an institute, according to the norms of the constitutions (see c. 631 §1). The tasks of the general chapter are, in particular:

- legislating for the institute,
- electing the supreme moderator,
- treating affairs of greater importance,
- protecting the patrimony of the institute, and
- promoting constant renewal.

The legislative power of the institute lies with the general chapter.[22] The supreme moderator of an institute is to be chosen by canonical election in accordance with the norm of the constitutions (see c. 625). The competence for this rests with the general chapter. In some institutes, other officials are also elected by the general chapter. In addition, the general chapter deals with affairs of greater importance, which are to be determined in the constitutions, and has the difficult task of protecting the patrimony, while at the same time promoting a constant renewal of the religious life in the institute (see PC 2). The constitutions are to define the composition and the extent of the authority of the general chapter. This includes determining the frequency of its convocation, whereas the general chapter must not be a permanent institution, nor must it be convened too frequently, so as not to interfere with the exercise of the ordinary governmental authority of the supreme moderator. The order to be observed in the celebration of the general chapter is to be established in the proper law (see c. 631 §2). Some persons are members ex officio, while others are elected or appointed as delegates according to the norms of the proper law. Universal law requires that the general chapter represent

[22] Formally, however, a general chapter does not enact laws but statutes, in the sense of c. 94.

the whole institute in order to become a true sign of unity in charity (see c. 631 §1). This requires an adequate representation of all the provinces or regions of the institute, as well as of all the areas of apostolate and activity. All members of the institute, as well as all provinces and houses, can directly address the general chapter with petitions and proposals in accordance with the provisions of the proper law. Usually, a special commission is appointed for this purpose, which deals with the submissions and places them on the agenda (see c. 631 §3).

There are chapters at each level of the institute. In addition to the general chapter at the level of the whole institute, there are provincial (or regional) chapters at the level of each province (or region) and house or conventual chapters at the level of each house. Further details concerning their nature, authority, composition, way of proceeding, and time of celebration are to be regulated by the proper law (see c. 632). The proper law may also provide for other similar assemblies, such as assemblies of several houses of a province or of several provinces of an institute (for example, from the same linguistic area).

While it is possible to hold councils digitally, provided that the proper law permits this, to hold chapters digitally is not allowed.[23] House or conventual chapters are not specifically mentioned in the circular letter of July 1, 2020, but the tenor of the text suggests that they cannot be held digitally either. Since all members of a house or conventual chapter are usually in the same house, this question is unlikely to arise in practice. In particular, this eliminates the possibility of legally absent members participating digitally in a house or conventual chapter. The only exception is when a chapter assumes the function of a council of the superior according to c. 627.

[23] See CICLSAL, "Circular Letter to General Moderators," July 1, 2020, no. 7: "[T]he Holy Father decreed . . . that no general or provincial chapters could be held by means of telecommunications, nor the combination of partial physical presence and partial presence through telecommunications, but only by means of physical presence."

The chapters, as participatory bodies, and the councils, as consultative bodies, express the concern and participation of all members for the good of the institute and the community (see c. 633 §1) and thus implement the principle of participation of all members in governance. All members are obliged to support the decisions legitimately taken. This gives a new emphasis to the understanding of obedience. Obedience now means not only obeying superiors but also accepting and supporting collectively made decisions.

Further reaching: Rose McDermott, "Governance in Religious Institutes: Structures of Participation and Representation: Canons 631–633," *Jur* 69 (2009): 442–71.

c) Temporal Goods and Their Administration (cc. 634–640)

As the administration of temporal goods is an important part of the governance, in the 1983 Code of Canon Law the norms relating to this area are included in a separate article in the chapter on the governance of institutes. Institutes, provinces, and houses lawfully erected are public juridic persons in canon law (see c. 116 §1). The temporal goods of public juridic persons are ecclesiastical goods[24] and are therefore governed by the canons of Book V of the Code of Canon Law (see c. 1257 §1). With regard to religious institutes, cc. 634–640 specify the norms of Book V concerning temporal goods (see c. 635 §1). In addition, the provisions of proper law apply as each institute has to establish norms concerning the use and administration of temporal goods with regard to its own patrimony and the poverty proper to it (see c. 635 §2). Last but not least, state laws must be observed, especially in the area of administration of temporal goods.

[24] This concerns only the temporal goods of juridic persons and not the temporal goods of the individual members (insofar as they are allowed to own temporal goods under the provisions of their proper law).

The Code of Canon Law does not contain a definition of the term "temporal goods." Temporal goods "are understood to include both material resources such as real property, whether moveable or immovable, and intangible or incorporeal things such as legal rights and obligations, titles, offices, annuities, as well as the more common cash, stocks, and bonds."[25] Institutes, provinces, and houses are capable of acquiring, possessing, administering, and alienating temporal goods, unless excluded or limited in the constitutions, which might be the case especially with mendicant orders (see c. 634 §1; c. 1255). All ecclesiastical goods are under the supreme authority of the pope,[26] but ownership remains with that juridic person that acquired them (see c. 1256; 1273). In this respect, ecclesiastical goods are distributed in a decentralized manner. Each juridic person is responsible for its own temporal goods, without prejudice to the supervisory rights of a higher authority and of the pope. The temporal goods of an institute are to be used to pursue its proper purposes as expressed in the patrimony (see c. 1254). Religious institutes "are to avoid any appearance of excess, immoderate wealth, and accumulation of goods" (c. 634 §2). They are called to give a common witness of charity and poverty, and to contribute, according to their means, to the needs of the church and the poor (see c. 640).

aa) Finance Officer (cc. 636–637)

The administration of temporal goods pertains to the superior who governs the institute, province, or house (see c. 1279 §1). In every institute and in every province governed by a major superior, there must be a finance officer (in some

[25] Rose McDermott, "Title II: Religious Institutes [cc. 606–709,]" in Beal et al., *New Commentary*, 797.

[26] For this reason, the periodic report on the status and life of an institute of consecrated life or society of apostolic life also has to include a section on the financial status and properties of the institute.

institutes called cellarer, oeconomus, or treasurer) who is different from the major superior and who is appointed according to the provisions of the proper law (c. 636 §1). In some institutes, the finance officer is appointed by the competent major superior; in others they are elected by the general, provincial, or conventual chapter. If possible, a finance officer distinct from the local superior is to be appointed in local communities (see c. 636 §1).[27] If in individual houses the offices of local superior and finance officer are held by the same person, adequate supervision of the house's finances shall be provided by other means.

Explicit qualification requirements for the position of finance officer may be laid down in the proper law. The administration of temporal goods in particular requires professional competence. Relevant qualifications and ongoing training are, therefore, essential. Universal law does not necessarily require the financial officer to be a member of the institute.[28] Unless otherwise provided by proper law, the position of financial officer may be filled with external parties (e.g., asset management agency, employees, or even qualified volunteers). In any case, the rights and obligations of both parties should be clearly defined in a contract. An alternative is to appoint a member of the institute as finance officer and to support them in their work through a financial advisory board composed of institute members and non-members.[29]

[27] This refers to non-autonomous houses. However, unless proper law provides otherwise, this provision may also be applied to autonomous houses. This interpretation makes it easier to fill the position of financial officer, especially in smaller communities.

[28] See Rose McDermott, "Canon 636: Finance Officer in a Religious Institute," *RRAO* 2020: 118–19.

[29] Experience with a financial advisory board in a German Benedictine monastery is discussed in Philipp Werner, *Klostermanagement im Team: Praktische Fallstudie über die Einrichtung eines Wirtschaftsrates in einer Benediktinerabtei, seine rechtliche Gestaltung und praktische Arbeit*, Kanonistische Reihe 34 (EOS, 2022).

The office of finance officer is an ecclesiastical office (see c. 145). The finance officer is entrusted with the administration of temporal goods under the direction of the superior and within the limits of universal law and proper law. Their essential duties are listed in c. 1284. Administrators of ecclesiastical goods are required to manage their responsibilities with the care and diligence of a prudent manager. This includes safeguarding goods from loss or damage and ensuring that ownership is legally protected, which may require arranging insurance. It is essential that they comply with both ecclesiastical and civil laws, as well as any specific conditions set by founders or donors, to prevent harm to the church. Administrators are also responsible for the timely and accurate collection and use of income, repayment of debts, and the prudent investment of surplus funds with the proper approvals. Proper record keeping is mandatory and includes maintaining organized financial records, preparing annual reports, and securely archiving important documents. Additionally, while preparing annual budgets is strongly encouraged, particular laws determine the specifics of this requirement. Proper law may provide for other duties of the financial officer. The relevant guidelines of the Apostolic See should also be followed.[30] Furthermore, institutes may develop guidelines for good management.

Autonomous monasteries referred to in c. 615 must give an account of their administration to the local ordinary once a year. In addition, the local ordinary has the right to be informed of the financial reports of a religious house of diocesan right in his territory (see c. 637). When and the manner in which the bishop is informed about the financial reports of these houses is to be determined in the diocese's proper law or in individual cases.

[30] See esp. CICLSAL, *Guidelines for the Administration of the Assets in Institutes of Consecrated Life and in Societies of Apostolic Life* (Libreria Editrice Vaticana, 2014); CICLSAL, *Economy at the Service of Charism and Mission* (Libreria Editrice Vaticana, 2018).

bb) Ordinary and Extraordinary Administration (c. 638 §§1–2)

A distinction is made between ordinary administration and extraordinary administration. Neither term is defined in universal law. What is to be regarded as ordinary administration and what as extraordinary administration is to be determined by proper law. In general, day-to-day business can be regarded as ordinary administration. This includes, for example, "meeting a payroll, depositing money in various accounts, overseeing an investment portfolio, and maintaining and repairing a building."[31] Within the limits of their function, the competent superior, the finance officer, and other officials designated for this in proper law validly perform acts of ordinary administration (see c. 638 §2). Proper law is to determine acts that exceed the limit and manner of ordinary administration and that are therefore acts of extraordinary administration. Furthermore, proper law is to determine what is necessary to place an act of extraordinary administration validly (see c. 638 §1). If the requirements established in proper law for performing acts of extraordinary administration are not met, the act is invalid in canon law.[32]

cc) Alienation (c. 638 §§3–4)

The alienation of stable patrimony (*patrimonium stabile*) requires special formalities for validity (see c. 638 §§3–4). Alienation is any legal act (e.g., sale or donation) by which ownership of property is transferred to another person (whether physical or juridic). This includes a transfer of property from one province to another of the same institute or from one autonomous house to another of the same institute. What applies to alienation also applies to any affair in which the patrimonial condition of a juridic person can worsen (see c.

[31] Rosemary Smith, "Chapter II: The Governance of Institutes [cc. 617–640]," in Beal et al., *New Commentary*, 802.

[32] This does not necessarily apply to state law. Such an act could still be valid under state law.

638 §3). The term of stable patrimony is not defined in the 1983 Code of Canon Law. The 2014 *Guidelines for the Administration of the Assets in Institutes of Consecrated Life and in Societies of Apostolic Life* define stable patrimony as "a permanent endowment (whether capital goods or income) of the juridic person for the purpose of facilitating the realization of the goals of the institute and insuring economic self-sufficiency."[33] The foundational endowment and donor-restricted gifts are, in general, considered elements of the stable patrimony.[34] Every religious institute is required to have stable patrimony.[35] Stable patrimony comes into existence through legitimate designation by the competent authority (see c. 1291).[36] The proper law of each institute is to determine which authority is competent to legitimately designate assets as stable patrimony.[37] This could be the superior with her or his council, the

[33] CICLSAL, *Guidelines for the Administration of the Assets*, 14–15.

[34] See CICLSAL, *Guidelines for the Administration of the Assets*, 15.

[35] See CICLSAL, *Guidelines for the Administration of the Assets*, 15–16; CICLSAL, *Economy at the Service of Charism and Mission*, no. 38.

[36] See CICLSAL, *Economy at the Service of Charism and Mission*, no. 40: "In choosing the assets to be included in the stable patrimony, it is necessary to consider what the assets are without which the juridical person would not have the means to reach its end. . . . [It is] not permitted to proceed with the assignment of the stable patrimony for the sole purpose of avoiding the requirements of the canon law on alienation. In fact, the establishment of this patrimony is for the purpose of protecting and guaranteeing these very assets."

[37] See CICLSAL, *Economy at the Service of Charism and Mission*, no. 38. For this purpose, a text such as the following should be inserted into the proper law of every institute: "The stable patrimony consists of all the immovable and movable property that by means of a specific assignment are destined to guarantee the economic security of the institute. For the goods of the entire institute, the General Chapter or the General Superior with the consent of his/her Council makes this assignment. For the assets of a province, as well as for the assets of a legitimately established house, the Provincial Chapter or other similar assemblies (cf. can. 632), or the Provincial Superior with the consent of his/her Council and confirmed by the Superior General makes this assignment." The naming of the competent authorities must be customized.

general, the provincial, or the conventual chapter. What is designated as stable patrimony must be recorded in the inventory according to c. 1283, 2°. Income from stable patrimony (e.g., interest or rent) is not considered stable patrimony, if it is not explicitly designated.

The written consent of the competent superior, with the approval of his or her council, is required for the validity[38] of alienation of stable patrimony and of any affair[39] that may deteriorate[40] the patrimonial condition of the institute (see c. 638 §3). For institutes of diocesan right, the written consent of the local ordinary is also required. For autonomous monasteries of nuns (see c. 615), on the other hand, the written permission of the major superior is required with the consent of the council or of the conventual chapter, depending on the value of the transaction and the opinion of the federal president (see CO 52).[41] If it concerns an affair that exceeds the amount[42] defined by the Apostolic See,[43] the permission of

[38] This does not necessarily apply to state law. An act invalid in canon law could still be valid under state law.

[39] Regardless of whether or not these affairs involve stable patrimony. See the response of May 14, 2020, of the Pontifical Council for Legislative Texts, prot. n. 16853/2020 (unpublished).

[40] This does not refer to an actual deterioration but to the mere possibility of deterioration.

[41] This exemption of c. 638 §4 has been approved *in forma specifica* by the pope.

[42] The basis is the actual purchase price, not the appraised value, although assets may not be sold for less than its appraised value (see c. 1294 §1).

[43] The Apostolic See may either adopt the amount defined by the bishops' conference (see c. 1292 §1) or define an own amount for religious institutes. In the United States, the amount depends on the number of Catholics in the diocese where the property or the goods concerned are located. If there are less than 500,000 Catholics, the amount is US$5,705,000, and if there are more than 500,000 Catholics, the amount is US$11,408,000 (see The Resource Center for Religious Institutes, "Alienation and Adverse Business Transaction Limits," www.trcri.org/page/alienation). For Canada, in 2025 the amount is CDN$6,770,461 and will be annually adjusted (see Canadian Conference of Catholic Bishops, Decree No. 38: Maximum Amount for Alienation of

the Apostolic See is also required. The permission of the Apostolic See is always required for the alienation of real estate if the established amount is exceeded, regardless of whether or not the real estate is stable patrimony.[44] In the case of real estate, it is also required that the local ordinary is informed of the intended alienation and that he gives his opinion on it, especially with regard to a possible acquisition for the pastoral use of the diocese.[45] In any case, the permission of the Apostolic See is required if it concerns things given to the church by vow or things precious for artistic or historical reasons, regardless of whether or not the things are stable patrimony or the established amount is exceeded.

Alienation of ecclesiastical goods or carrying out an act of administration over them without the prescribed consultation, consent, or permission, or without another requirement imposed by law, is punishable by canon law (see c. 1376 §1,2°).

dd) Liability for Debts and Obligations (c. 639)

A basic principle is that each juridic person must answer for its own debts and obligations, even if they were contracted with the permission of the superiors (see c. 639 §1). If a member has entered into a contract in the name of the institute by mandate of the superior, the institute must answer. If a member has entered into a contract concerning their own goods with the permission of their superior, the member must answer (see c. 639 §2). If a member has entered a contract without any permission of their superiors, they must answer

---

Church Property, www.cccb.ca/letter/decree-no-38-maximum-amount-alienation-church-property).

44 See CICLSAL, *Economy at the Service of Charism and Mission*, no. 81. This was confirmed in a response of the Pontifical Council for Legislative Texts of December 3, 2018, prot. n. 16489/2018, in *RRAO* 2021: 14.

45 See CICLSAL, Circular Letter *Amministrazione dei beni temporali negli Istituti religiosi*, December 21, 2004, prot. no. 971/2004, in *Leges Ecclesiae*, vol. X: *Leges annis 2000–2006 editae*, ed. Dominicus Andrés Gutiérrez, no. 6212, col. 17976–17978 (Editiones Instituti Iuridici Claretiani, 2010).

themself; the institute is not liable (see c. 639 §3). In the latter two cases, a member is personally liable with their private property, if such property exists (see c. 668).

Superiors are to take care not to allow debts to be contracted unless it is certain that the interest can be paid out of ordinary income and that the capital sum can be repaid by legitimate amortization within a not too long time (see c. 639 §5).

Further reading: John P. Beal, "Charism, Mission, and Canon Law: Management as Ministry," *StudCan* 55 (2021): 169–94; Congregation for Institutes of Consecrated Life and Societies of Apostolic Life, *Guidelines for the Administration of the Assets in Institutes of Consecrated Life and in Societies of Apostolic Life* (Libreria Editrice Vaticana, 2014); Congregation for Institutes of Consecrated Life and Societies of Apostolic Life, *Economy at the Service of Charism and Mission* (Libreria Editrice Vaticana, 2018); Maria-Stella Joseph Ekot, *Administration of Temporal Goods of Religious Institutes According to the Teachings of the Church and the Codes of Canon Law* (Pontificia Università Gregoriana, 2022); Robert Geisinger, "Some Ongoing Considerations in Canon Law for Treasurers General of Religious Institutes," *PRC* 95 (2006): 227–59; Varghese Koluthara, "Religious and the Administration of Temporal Goods," *Iustitia: Dharmaram Journal of Canon Law* 9 (2018): 95–108; Rose McDermott, "The Financial Administrator of a Religious Institute," *RRAO* 1997: 58–59; Rose McDermott, "Canon 636: Finance Officer in a Religious Institute," *RRAO* 2020: 118–19; Francis G. Morrisey, "The Directory for the Administration of Temporal Goods in Religious Institutes," in *Unico Ecclesiae Servitio: Canonical Studies Presented to Germain Lesage, O.M.I., on the Occasion of His 75th Birthday and of the 50th Anniversary of His Presbyterial Ordination*, ed. Michel Thériault (Faculty of Canon Law, Saint Paul University, 1991), 227–59; Francis G. Morrisey, "New Directives from the Holy See on the Administration of Temporal Goods for Institutes of Consecrated Life and Societies of Apostolic Life," *Studies in Church Law* 14 (2019): 227–58; John A. Renken, "The Stable Patrimony of Public Juridic Persons," *Jur* 70 (2010): 131–62; John A. Renken, "Acts of Extraordinary Administration of Ecclesiastical Goods in Book V of the CIC," *StudCan* 49 (2015): 577–96; Yuji Sugawara, "Amministrazione e alienazione dei beni temporali degli Istituti religiosi nel Codice (can. 638)," *PRC* 97 (2008): 251–82.

3. Admission of Candidates and the Formation of Members (cc. 641–661)

The admission of candidates and the formation of members are particularly important for a religious institute, as this is where the foundation stone is laid for the passing on of its own patrimony and thus for the future of the institute. Initial formation in a religious institute is divided into different stages. At the beginning there is a preparatory period (see c. 597 §2), usually called candidacy or aspirancy, followed by postulancy, to be defined in more detail by the institute's proper law. This is followed by admission to the novitiate. Profession is initially made for a limited period (juniorate) before final admission to the institute in perpetual profession. After this initial formation, formation continues in a lifelong process.

The initial formation for nuns is regulated in *Cor Orans* 250–89. It is divided into the stages of aspirancy (1–2 years), postulancy (1–2 years), novitiate (2 years), and juniorate (at least 5 years). Initial formation for nuns, therefore, lasts at least nine years. The duration of the juniorate can be extended, but the total duration of initial formation for nuns should not exceed twelve years.

Further reading: Congregation for Institutes of Consecrated Life and Societies of Apostolic Life, *Potissimum Institutioni:*

On Formation in Religious Institutes, February 2, 1990, www.vatican.va/roman_curia/congregations/ccscrlife/documents/rc_con_ccscrlife_doc_02021990_directives-on-formation_en.html; Congregation for Institutes of Consecrated Life and Societies of Apostolic Life, *On Inter-Institute Collaboration for Formation*, December 8, 1998, www.vatican.va/roman_curia/congregations/ccscrlife/documents/rc_con_ccscrlife_doc_08121998_inter-formation_en.html.

a) Admission to the Novitiate (cc. 641–645)

The novitiate is preceded by a preparatory period, since no one can be admitted without suitable preparation (see c. 597 §2). The details are left to proper law. As a rule, the preparatory period is divided into candidacy (also called aspirancy) as a time of mutual acquaintance, and postulancy as a time during which the candidate lives, prays, and works together with the community to become more closely acquainted with it and its apostolate, engages in the spirituality of the institute, and, if necessary, deepens their basic religious formation and human maturity. The community, for its part, has the opportunity to get to know the candidate and to discern whether he or she will fit into the community and be able to support its apostolate. It is up to the proper law to establish the criteria for admission to the preparatory period. In principle, no one should be admitted who does not meet the criteria for admission to the novitiate or who cannot be expected to meet them by the time the novitiate is scheduled to begin. For nuns, an aspirancy and a postulancy of at least twelve months each are prescribed (CO 268, 275). The period of both aspirancy and postulancy may be extended at the discretion of the major superior with the consent of her council, but not beyond two years in each case.

The right to admit candidates to the novitiate belongs to the competent major superior according to proper law (see c. 641). The basic requirements for admission to the novitiate are given in c. 597:

- being a Catholic
- right intention
- possession of the qualities required by universal law and proper law
- not prevented by any impediment

According to universal law, the following qualities are required (see c. 642):

- required age
- necessary physical and mental health
- suitable character
- sufficient maturity

The necessary health is usually verified by a medical examination. Standardized tests, which are carried out and evaluated by a psychologist or psychiatrist, are usually used to determine suitable character and sufficient maturity.[46] The psychologist should discuss the results with the candidate and the superior. The privacy of the candidate must always be protected (see c. 220). The final decision whether the candidate is of suitable character and sufficient maturity to be admitted rests with the competent superior. The proper law may establish further requirements for admission to the novitiate.

Impediments to valid admission are listed in c. 643 §1. The following qualities prevent candidates from being validly admitted:

- being below seventeen years of age
- being a spouse, while the marriage continues to exist

[46] For a list of which medical reports and psychological evaluation reports should be obtained, see Donna Miller and Eileen C. Jaramillo, eds. *Procedural Handbook for Institutes of Consecrated Life and Societies of Apostolic Life* (CLSA, 2021), 78–79.

- being currently bound by a bond to an institute of consecrated life or incorporated in a society of apostolic life
- entering the institute induced by force, grave fear, or malice, or being one whom a superior, induced in the same way, has received
- concealment of incorporation in an institute of consecrated life or in a society of apostolic life

The proper law of an institute can establish other impediments, even for validity of admission, or can attach conditions (c. 643 §2).

According to universal law, the minimum age for valid admission is seventeen (see c. 643 §1,1°). This is very young, especially in North American culture, in order to have the sufficient maturity. A higher age may be provided for in the proper law. The proper law may also provide for a maximum age.

Consecrated life and married life are mutually exclusive. Therefore, no one can be validly admitted to the novitiate while married (see c. 643 §1,2°). Candidates who have been married and who are divorced are no longer an exception. Divorce has no influence on the validity of the marriage in canon law. In this case, an ecclesiastical declaration of nullity of the marriage is required before admission to the novitiate.[47] If a declaration of nullity is not possible—for example, because there are no grounds for nullity—it remains possible to request

[47] See Clinton J. Doskey, "Declaration of Nullity: Its Effect on Admission to Clerical and Religious Life," *CLSA Proceedings* 47 (1985): 115–23; Rose McDermott, "Admission to the Noviciate with Declaration of Nullity," *RRAO* 1998: 58–59. For further practical information on a declaration of nullity, see United States Conference of Catholic Bishops, "Annulment," www.usccb.org/topics/marriage-and-family-life-ministries/annulment

a dispensation from the Apostolic See.[48] The Apostolic See is always competent to grant the dispensation, for institutes of diocesan right as well as for institutes of pontifical right. The competent superior addresses the request for dispensation to the Dicastery for Institutes of Consecrated Life and Societies of Apostolic Life, and submits the following documents:

- petition of the candidate, with indication of the reasons for the request
- curriculum vitae of the candidate
- brief report on the reasons for the breakdown of the marriage and whether there are still legal or moral obligations towards the spouse
- brief report on any children born of the marriage and their ages, and whether there are any legal or moral obligations towards them
- declaration before the local ordinary and the chancellor of the diocesan curia that the spouse agrees to the candidate's admission to a religious institute and that they definitively renounce all rights arising from the marriage
- notarized declaration by both spouses of final separation by mutual consent and of the obligation not to assert any claims of a personal or material nature arising from the marriage
- documents regarding civil divorce
- letter of recommendation from the local ordinary or parish priest regarding the candidate's right intention and sufficient maturity

[48] See Victor G. D'Souza, "Admission of Married Catholics into Religious Institutes," *Studies in Church Law* 6 (2010): 403–13; Rose McDermott, "Admission to the Novitiate: Canon 643 §1,2°: Impediment of Existing Marriage Bond," in Cogan, *Selected Issues in Religious Law*, 160–62.

- confirmation by the competent major superior regarding the intention to admit the candidate to the novitiate and documentation of the decision-making process in the community

The dicastery may also request a decree of permanent separation from the local ordinary (see cc. 1151–1155, 1692–1696) to ensure that there was a legitimate reason for separation (see c. 1153 §1). If both a declaration of nullity and the granting of a dispensation are not possible, the alternative is to be admitted as a conventual (or claustral) oblate, if the proper law so provides. In any case, before admitting a divorced person, the reasons for the breakdown of the marriage should be asked, in order to be able to assess whether these reasons have an effect on the character and human maturity required for admission to the institute.

Anyone who is a member of an institute of consecrated life or a society of apostolic life cannot be validly admitted to the novitiate (see c. 643 §1,2°). In this case, a transfer according to cc. 684–685 is to be carried out.

An act placed out of grave fear, unjustly inflicted, or placed out of malice is in principle legally valid but can be rescinded through the sentence of a judge (see c. 125 §1). Canon 643 §1,4° departs from this principle. In practice, the case of malice is particularly relevant. If a candidate, for example, conceals relevant information, admission to the novitiate would be invalid.

According to c. 542,1° of the 1917 Code, anyone who had previously been a professed member of a religious institute was not validly admitted to the novitiate. In the 1983 Code, this provision was modified (see c. 643 §1,5°). A previous profession as such is no longer an impediment, but only the concealment of a previous incorporation into an institute of consecrated life or a society of apostolic life. This concerns profession in a religious institute, commitment of sacred bonds in a secular institute, or incorporation into a society of apostolic life. Postulancy, novitiate, or other initial probation are not included. If the candidate discloses their previous incorporation, there is no impediment. In practice, it is important for the assessment of a candidate's suitability to know whether they have previously been incorporated into an institute of consecrated life or a society of apostolic life and to know the reasons for their departure or dismissal.

These impediments affect the validity of admission to the novitiate. If there is an impediment and a candidate is nevertheless admitted, the admission to the novitiate is invalid and thus also a subsequent profession. Proper law can establish further impediments, also for validity (see c. 643 §2), for example, lacking a required level of education or being bound by natural obligations toward another party (such as parents in need of care).

Admission to the novitiate is illicit in the following cases (see c. 644):

- admission of a secular cleric without consultation with his proper ordinary
- admission of one who is burdened with debts and is unable to repay them

Secular clerics are priests and deacons incardinated in a particular church or personal prelature. Before admitting them, the superior must consult the ordinary. The ordinary has no right to object. After consultation with the ordinary, the decision on admission rests with the superior.

In order to protect the institute from harm, no one may be admitted who has debts that they cannot pay.[49] In the United

[49] See Eileen C. Jaramillo, "Canon 644: Addressing Debts before Entering a Religious Institute," *RRAO* 2010: 110–13. If a candidate conceals their debts, this is a case of fraud, and their admission to the novitiate would be invalid (see c. 643 §1,4°).

States, student loan debt of candidates is therefore a problem.[50] Institutes should develop a policy in this regard. The institute may agree to pay the monthly installments and to pay off the debt in full after perpetual profession.[51] Alternatively, a candidate could try to raise funds to pay off the debt, or, if possible, apply for student loan deferment.

Admitting a candidate contrary to c. 644 would make the admission illicit but not invalid.

Before a candidate may be admitted to the novitiate, the following documents must be presented (see c. 645 §§1–2):

- proof of baptism and confirmation
- proof of free status
- if it concerns the admission of clerics: testimony of the local ordinary
- if it concerns the admission of those who have been admitted to a seminary: testimony of the rector of the seminary
- if it concerns the admission of those who have been admitted to another institute of consecrated life or society of apostolic life: testimony of the major superior

Proof of baptism, confirmation, and free status is provided by a certificate of baptism from the parish, providing informa-

[50] See Amy Hereford, "Canon 644: Education Loans of Those Entering Religious Communities," *RRAO* 2010: 114–15; Kathleen A. Mahoney, ed. *Handbook on Educational Debt and Vocations to Religious Life* (National Religious Vocation Conference, 2013), www.nrvc.net/download/1532/educational_debt_handbook_3-2-14.pdf.

[51] This decision requires a great deal of discretion on the part of the institute. Well-educated candidates should not be easily rejected because of student loan debt. On the other hand, it is important to avoid accepting candidates who simply want their student loan debt to be paid off and leave. For a sample agreement between the institute and a candidate regarding student loans debt, see Miller and Jaramillo, *Procedural Handbook*, 966.

tion from the parish sacramental register. If the certificate does not record a marriage, this is considered proof of free status.

Other proof of a candidate's suitability and freedom from impediments may be required by proper law (see c. 645 §3), for example, letter(s) of recommendation, proof of education, or criminal background check.

If he deems it necessary, the superior may seek further information, even under secrecy (see c. 645 §4). Since such an investigation may involve sensitive matters, the superior must be careful not to harm the candidate's good reputation and to respect their right to privacy (see c. 220).

Further reading: Nancy Bauer, "The Lengthening Duration of Initial Formation in Religious Institutes: Historical-Canonical Overview," *StudCan* 55 (2021): 147–67; Clinton J. Doskey, "Declaration of Nullity: Its Effect on Admission to Clerical and Religious Life," *CLSA Proceedings* 47 (1985): 115–23; Victor G. D'Souza, "Admission of Married Catholics into Religious Institutes," *Studies in Church Law* 6 (2010): 403–13; Amy Hereford, "Canon 644: Education Loans of Those Entering Religious Communities," *RRAO* 2010: 114–15; Eileen C. Jaramillo, "Canon 644: Addressing Debts before Entering a Religious Institute," *RRAO* 2010: 110–13; Kathleen A. Mahoney, ed., *Handbook on Educational Debt and Vocations to Religious Life* (National Religious Vocation Conference, 2013), www.nrvc.net/download/1532/educational_debt_handbook_3-2-14.pdf; Francis J. Marini, "Readmission of Former Member of Religious Institute," *RRAO* 2006: 174–76; Rose McDermott, "Admission to the Novitiate: Canon 643 §1,2°: Impediment of Existing Marriage Bond," in Cogan, *Selected Issues in Religious Law*, 160–62; Rose McDermott, "Admission to the Novitiate with Declaration of Nullity," *RRAO* 1998: 58–59; Diego Eugenio Pombo Oncins, "La responsabilità dei Superiori nell'ammissione all'Istituto (cann. 597, 641–645)," *PRC* 107 (2015): 591–610; Therese G. Sullivan, "Canons 125; 205; 219;

573-606; 641-661; 675: Suitability of Persons with Transsexualism," *RRAO* 2019: 39–44.

b) The Novitiate and Formation of Novices (cc. 646–653)

The formation of novices has a spiritual and a practical dimension (see c. 646). The spiritual dimension consists in better understanding their own divine vocation and the vocation proper to the institute, and in forming the mind and heart in the spirit of the institute. The practical side of the formation of novices is that the novices experience the institute's way of life and that their suitability and right intention can be proven.

Autonomous houses usually have their own novitiate. In institutes with non-autonomous houses, there is usually one house designated as novitiate in each province. The erection, transfer, and suppression of a novitiate house is the responsibility of the supreme moderator of an institute with the consent of his council by written decree (see c. 647 §1). In order to be valid, the novitiate must take place in a duly designated novitiate house (see c. 647 §2). In exceptional cases, the major superior of an institute, with the consent of his or her council, may allow the novitiate to take place in another house of the institute under the direction of an approved religious who acts in the place of the director of novices. The major superior may also permit novices to spend certain periods of time in another house of the institute designated by him or her (see c. 647 §3). This is an opportunity for the novices to get to know the communities of other houses and their apostolate as part of their formation. At a time when the number of novices is decreasing and it may be difficult to find suitable formators, collaboration among institutes in the area of formation is important, including through inter-institute formation centers.[52]

[52] See CICLSAL, *On Inter-Institute Collaboration for Formation*, nos. 4–18. Also Jordan F. Hite, "The Inter-Community Novitiate," in Cogan, *Selected Issues in Religious Law*, 154–59.

For the novitiate to be valid, it must last twelve months[53] (see c. 648 §1). This is called the "canonical year." In monasteries of nuns, the novitiate lasts two years, the second year being the canonical year (see CO 279). The canonical year must be spent in the community of the novitiate itself, without prejudice to the above-mentioned exception in c. 647 §3. The constitutions of an institute may prescribe apostolic exercises outside the community of the novitiate for the formation of novices (see c. 648 §2). However, the time of these exercises may not be included in the minimum period of twelve months prescribed for the novitiate, but the novitiate is to be extended by the duration of these exercises. Since the twelve months of the canonical year do not necessarily have to be consecutive, the novitiate may be interrupted by such exercises. Proper law may provide for a longer period for the novitiate, but the novitiate must not be extended beyond two years (see c. 648 §3). Except in the case of a stay in another house of the institute authorized by the superior (see c. 647 §3) and in the case of apostolic exercises (see c. 648 §2), the time of which must in any case be added to the twelve months of the canonical year, an absence from the novitiate house of more than three months, with or without interruption, renders the novitiate invalid (see c. 649 §1). In this case, the novitiate must be repeated. An absence of up to fifteen days does not affect the validity of the novitiate. Absences of more than fifteen days and up to three months must be made up. The competent major superior may anticipate the first profession after the novitiate by a maximum of fifteen days (see c. 649 §2).

For the formation of novices, a guideline on formation (*ratio institutionis*) is to be drawn up in every institute. Novices

[53] The 1917 Code of Canon Law set the minimum duration of the novitiate as a complete and unbroken year (see c. 555 §1,2° CIC/1917), while the 1983 Code prescribes a period of twelve months, not necessarily consecutive. As, according to c. 202 §1, a month is considered in law as a period of thirty days, the minimum duration is now 360 days.

are formed under the guidance of a director of novices (see c. 650 §1). The director of novices is under the authority of the competent major superior for the governance of the novices (see c. 650 §2), not under the authority of the local superior of the novitiate house. Universal law establishes only the following criteria for the director of novices. They must be a member of the institute who has professed perpetual vows and has been legitimately designated (see c. 651 §1). The director of novices need not necessarily be a priest, even in clerical institutes, if this is not required by proper law. Contrary to the 1917 Code, the 1983 Code does not specify a minimum age or minimum period of time that must have elapsed after perpetual profession. These and other criteria may, however, be established by proper law. The director of novices may be given assistants who help them in the formation of novices (see c. 651 §2). This does not constitute collegial direction of the novitiate. The assistants are under the authority of the director of novices. The director of novices and their assistants must be carefully prepared for their task (see c. 651 §3). They should not be impeded by other duties from carrying out their function in a stable and fruitful manner, which is a particular challenge for smaller institutes. The formation of novices should include the following areas (see c. 652 §2):

- cultivation of human and Christian virtues
- prayer
- *lectio divina*
- cultivation of the worship of God in the liturgy
- cultivation of a life consecrated to God and humanity in Christ through the evangelical counsels
- deepening understanding of the character and spirit, purpose and discipline, history and life of the institute

In order to respond faithfully to their vocation, novices should collaborate actively with their director (see c. 652 §3). All the members of the institute should take care that they, in their turn, cooperate in the work of the formation of the novices by the example of their life and of their prayer (see c. 652 §4). The time of the canonical year is intended exclusively for the formation of the novitiate; therefore, during the canonical year the novices may not be engaged in studies or work that do not directly serve the formation of the novitiate (see c. 652 §5). This means that novices may not be used to fill personnel gaps in the novitiate house. Similarly, during the canonical year, they may not engage in professional training or university studies, although this does not preclude them from taking certain courses at a university as part of their novitiate formation. The director of novices and their assistants are responsible for discerning the vocation of the novices (see c. 652 §1).

A novice is not bound by vows. They are therefore free to leave the institute at any time, and the competent authority may dismiss[54] them at any time in accordance with the provisions of proper law (see c. 653 §1). Universal law does not prescribe a specific form for the dismissal of a novice. The reason for dismissal need not be given from a legal point of view, if it is not required by proper law, but this would not be good administrative practice.[55] Ideally, novices should be informed of the goals of the novitiate and the criteria for admission to the profession before they enter the novitiate. During the novitiate, the novice director should periodically

[54] What the 1983 Code refers to as the dismissal of a novice is not a dismissal in the strict legal sense. Since a novice has not yet made profession and is therefore not yet incorporated into the institute, they cannot be dismissed from the institute in the legal sense. Nevertheless, as in the Code, the term "dismissal" is used here.

[55] See Catherine Darcy, "Right to Withhold or Obligation to Disclose Reasons for Dismissal of a Novice or Extending the Novitiate," *RRAO* 1995: 52–55

evaluate with the novice the novice's fulfillment of the admission criteria. If a novice does not fulfill the criteria, the responsible superior should inform the novice in writing of his dismissal from the novitiate or non-admission to the profession, giving reasons. This would contribute to greater transparency. If a novice has lawfully completed the novitiate and then left the institute, it is possible, under the conditions of c. 690, to readmit them a later date without the obligation of repeating the novitiate.[56] At the end of the novitiate, the novice must either be admitted to first profession or dismissed from the institute (see c. 653 §2). If there is still doubt about the suitability of the novice, the major superior may extend the novitiate in accordance with the provisions of proper law, but not beyond six months. If the proper law provides for a two-year novitiate, the major superior may also extend this two-year novitiate by a maximum of six months, so that, taking into account c. 648 §3, the novitiate may last a maximum of two and a half years.

Further reading: Catherine Darcy, "Right to Withhold or Obligation to Disclose Reasons for Dismissal of a Novice or Extending the Novitiate," *RRAO* 1995: 52–55; Evaldo X. Gomes, "Readmissão de candidatos à vida religiosa segundo o cânone 690 do Código de Direito Canônico," *Direito e pastoral* 17 (2003): 45–53; Jordan F. Hite, "The Inter-Community Novitiate," in Cogan, *Selected Issues in Religious Law*, 154–59; Francis J. Marini, "Readmission of Former Member of Religious Institute," RRAO 2006: 174–76; Rose McDermott, "Purpose and Place of the Novitiate: Canons 646–647," in Cogan, *Selected Issues in Religious Law*, 150–53.

[56] See Evaldo X. Gomes, "Readmissão de candidatos à vida religiosa segundo o cânone 690 do Código de Direito Canônico," *Direito e pastoral* 17 (2003): 45–53; Francis J. Marini, "Readmission of Former Member of Religious Institute," *RRAO* 2006: 174–76.

c) Religious Profession (cc. 654–658)

By profession, members of religious institutes undertake the observance of the three evangelical counsels through a public vow (see c. 654), that is, a vow received by the legitimate superior in the name of the church (see c. 1192 §1). The formula for profession is to be laid down in the constitutions. The profession has both a spiritual and a juridical dimension. Spiritually, it is an act of worship in which the professed enters into a special relationship with God and commits themself totally to Him. Juridically, profession creates a new status in the church for the professed, with the rights and obligations that come with that status.[57] In addition, the professed person is incorporated into a particular institute, so that the profession has a contractual character that binds the religious and the institute. In particular, the professed person submits to the full availability of the institute according to universal law and proper law. The institute undertakes to provide for the professed person (see c. 670). When a cleric makes perpetual profession, he is excardinated from his former particular church and incardinated into the institute (see c. 268 §2).

A profession can be temporary or perpetual with regard to its duration and simple or solemn with regard to its legal effects. Temporary profession is a relatively recent institution. It was introduced by Pius IX on March 19, 1857, with the encyclical *Neminem Latet*,[58] which required that simple vows be taken for three years after the novitiate before perpetual profession could be made. This was to allow for another period of discernment after the novitiate. The 1983 Code of Canon Law, in general, no longer distinguishes between religious with

[57] The rights and obligations arising from the profession are governed in particular by cc. 662–672 and by the proper law.

[58] Pope Pius IX, "Litterae encyclicae *Neminem latet*," March 19, 1857, in *Collectanea in usum secretariae Sacrae Congregationis Episcoporum et Regularium*, ed. Giuseppe Andrea Bizzarri (Tipografia Poliglotta 1885), 853–55.

simple and solemn vows. In universal law, the distinction only plays a role with regard to the right to property. Those who make solemn profession renounce all possessions; those who make simple profession do not necessarily do so. In the proper law of various institutions, however, the distinction has been preserved.

After the novitiate, temporary profession is to be made for a period to be determined by proper law (see c. 655). It must be for a minimum of three years and a maximum of six years, although it may be divided into several periods.[59] At the end of the period for which the profession was made, the temporary profession may be renewed in accordance with the provisions of proper law, but the total duration of the temporary profession may not exceed nine years (see c. 657 §2). Nuns are required to make temporary profession for an initial period of three years and to renew it annually until the completion of five years (see CO 287). For the validity of temporary profession, the following is required (see c. 656):

- minimum age of eighteen years
- novitiate has been validly completed
- admission has been given freely by the competent superior with the vote[60] of the council
- profession is expressed and made without force, grave fear, or malice
- profession is received by a legitimate superior personally or through another person

[59] The first profession does not necessarily have to be for three years at a time. It is also possible to make profession for one year and to extend it twice for one year each time, or to make profession for two years and to extend it for one year each time. In any case, the total period must be at least three years.

[60] Whether it is a consultative vote or a deliberative vote is to be determined in proper law.

The minimum age is determined by the minimum age for entry into the novitiate. A higher minimum age, as well as a maximum age, may be established by proper law. Furthermore, the novitiate must have been validly completed. An invalid novitiate would lead to an invalid profession. Consent to profession must be freely given, both by the superior and by the candidate. Consent given under force, great fear, or malice would render the profession invalid (see c. 125). The profession must be made expressly. It is not possible to make an implicit profession, for example, by merely wearing the religious habit of the institute and observing the external rules of the institute. The profession must be received by the responsible superior or by a person legitimately delegated by him. The profession has the character of a contract, so that it cannot be made unilaterally, but requires acceptance. When the period for which profession was made has elapsed, the religious must either be admitted to renewal of profession or to perpetual profession, or they must depart (see c. 657 §1).

For the validity of perpetual profession, the following is required (see c. 658):

- minimum age of twenty-one years
- admission has been given freely by the competent superior with the vote[61] of the council
- profession is expressed and made without force, grave fear, or malice
- profession is received by a legitimate superior personally or through another person
- previous temporary profession of at least three years

[61] Also in this case, whether it is a consultative vote or a deliberative vote is to be determined in proper law.

The minimum age is determined by the minimum age for admission to the novitiate and the minimum age for temporary profession. A higher minimum age, as well as a maximum age, may be established by proper law. Consent to the profession must be given explicitly and freely, both by the superior and by the candidate. Consent given under force, great fear, or malice would invalidate the profession (see c. 125). The profession must be received by the competent superior or by a person legitimately delegated by them. Perpetual profession must be preceded by temporary profession of at least three years. The superior may, for a just cause, anticipate perpetual profession by a maximum of three months (see c. 657 §3).

The competent major superior, after having heard the council, can for a just cause exclude a religious from making a subsequent profession when the period of temporary profession has been elapsed (see c. 689 §1).[62] A just cause may be that the religious is unable[63] or unwilling to live the observance of the institute or that they do not integrate themself into the community. Physical or mental illness that, in the opinion of experts,[64] renders a religious unfit to lead the life of the institute, constitutes a just cause for not admitting to renewal of profession or to perpetual profession, unless the illness was

[62] See Jacinta Auma Opondo, *Temporary Profession and Exclusion from Subsequent Profession (cann. 655; 689): Theological-juridical Study*, Tesi gregoriana / Serie diritto canonico 106 (Editrice Pontificia Università Gregoriana, 2017).

[63] Life as a Carthusian monk, for example, is physically and mentally demanding. It may be that a candidate is simply not capable of meeting these demands.

[64] "The assessment of the candidate's lack of suitability due to infirmity is entrusted to experts; the judgment on the suitability to lead the life of the Institute is entrusted to the superiors" (CICLSAL, *The Gift of Fidelity, The Joy of Perseverance: Manete in dilectione mea (Jn 15:9): Guidelines* [Libreria Editrice Vaticana, 2020; also available at https://www.vitaconsacrata.va/content/dam/vitaconsacrata/LibriPPDF/Francese/dono-della-fedelta_ING_testo_stampa-1.pdf] [hereafter, GoF], 76).

contracted through the negligence of the institute or through work performed in the institute (see c. 689 §2). If a religious becomes insane[65] during temporary profession, they cannot be dismissed from the institute, even if they are incapable of subsequent profession (see c. 689 §3). In practice, however, it will be difficult to distinguish between becoming mentally ill and becoming insane. These could be cases where someone is unable to make a decision for or against profession for psychological reasons. Such a religious would be suspended in the state of temporary profession and would have to receive the necessary treatment until they are again able to make a decision. Non-admission to subsequent profession is to be made by written decree of the competent superior, which must at least give a summary of the reasons (see c. 51). An administrative recourse against the non-admission is possible.

d) Formation of Religious (cc. 659–661)

The novitiate is the basic formation. After first profession, the formation of religious is to be perfected "so that they lead the proper life of the institute more fully and carry out its mission more suitably" (c. 659 §1). The type of formation necessary depends on the patrimony and apostolate of an institute. In monastic orders a different kind of formation is required than in apostolic institutes. In any case, formation must be "spiritual and apostolic, doctrinal and at the same time practical" (c. 660 §1). Formation is not limited to the acquisition of knowledge and practical skills but also includes spiritual and human growth. Each institute is to set up directives and regulations on formation (*ratio institutionis*), as it is also required for the novitiate (see c. 650 §1). The formation of candidates for the priesthood is governed by universal law and by the institute's own program of studies (*ratio studiorum*)

[65] The Latin word for "insane" in c. 689 §3 is "*amens*," which literally means: to lose one's mind.

that is to be established by each institute (see c. 659 §3).[66] The program of studies is intended to ensure that the formation is systematic. However, there should also be sufficient opportunity to adapt the formation to the capacity of the individual religious. Formation should also be spiritual and directed to the apostolic work specific to the institute. Theoretical and practical elements are complementary. Whenever possible, formation should include the acquisition of degrees and titles (see c. 660 §1). Religious in formation should have sufficient time and energy to devote to their formation. Therefore, during the period of formation, they should not be assigned ministries and tasks that may impede their formation (see c. 660 §2).

Formation does not end with perpetual profession. Religious should continue their formation throughout their lives. Superiors should give them the necessary help and time for this (see c. 661). In a certain sense, it is possible to speak of a right and a duty to continue formation, but always according to the individual circumstances of each person and taking into account the possibilities and capacities of the institute and of the religious. Conferences of major superiors should develop programs for the ongoing formation of religious.

Further reading: Marren Rose A. Awiti, "Formation during the Period of Temporary Vows According to the 1983 Code and the Subsequent Apostolic See Documents," *StudCan* 51 (2017): 391–439; Thomas F. Purcell, *The Training of Members of Religious Institutes for Ordained Ministry According to the*

[66] See Thomas F. Purcell, *The Training of Members of Religious Institutes for Ordained Ministry According to the Current Law of the Church*, Canon Law Studies 537 (Catholic University of America Press, 2001). The programs of priestly formation of the bishops' conferences may serve as an orientation guide for religious institutes. See Canadian Conference of Catholic Bishops, *Program for Priestly Formation (Ratio formationis sacerdotalis nationalis) for English-speaking Canada* (CCCB, 2022); United States Conference of Catholic Bishops, *Program of Priestly Formation in the United States of America*, 6th ed. (USCCB, 2022).

Current Law of the Church, Canon Law Studies 537 (Catholic University of America Press, 2001); United States Conference of Catholic Bishops, *Program of Priestly Formation in the United States of America*, 6th ed. (USCCB, 2022).

4. Rights and Obligations of Institutes and Their Members (cc. 662–672)

The rights and obligations of the institutes and their members arising from profession are laid down in particular in cc. 662–672. These norms are formulated as obligations. Implicitly, an obligation leads to a right to fulfill that obligation. The obligation to an annual period of spiritual retreat, for example, constitutes implicitly the right to receive all necessary means (free time, travel expenses, etc.) to fulfill that obligation. Universal law formulates only a few general principles. It is left to proper law to concretize these principles according to the patrimony of the institute. The proper law may contain further rights and duties.

a) Spiritual Life (cc. 662–664)

The supreme rule of life for a religious is the following of Christ as expressed in the Gospel and concretized in the constitutions according to the patrimony of the institute (see c. 662). Different institutes cultivate their own forms of worship according to their own tradition. Canons 663–664 list various forms of spiritual worship recommended to all religious:

- contemplation of divine things
- assiduous union with God in prayer
- daily participation in the Eucharistic celebration and reception of the Body of Christ, if possible
- adoration
- *lectio divina*

- Liturgy of the Hours according to the prescripts of proper law
- veneration of the Mother of God, including through the rosary
- annual spiritual retreat
- daily examination of conscience
- frequent reception of the sacrament of penance

These points reflect basic spiritual practices common to all religious, regardless of personal piety or the spiritual orientation of the institute. Canons 663–664, except for the obligation to celebrate the liturgy of the hours, contain directory provisions.[67] The contemplation of divine things shall lead to a constant union with God in prayer. It is a state rather than an act of worship. The religious should direct their whole life to God, not only practicing constant prayer but becoming a prayer with their whole person. Daily attendance at Mass and daily reception of Communion are recommended. This can be a problem especially for contemplative women's monasteries, if they cannot find enough priests to celebrate daily Mass in their monastery. Religious should also devote themselves to adoration and *lectio divina*. Sufficient time for this should be included in the schedule of each community. The only explicit obligation mentioned in the list concerns the Liturgy of the Hours. The extent of this obligation is regulated by proper law. For religious who are clerics, the obligation also arises from c. 276 § 2,3°. In addition, devotion to the Mother of God, including through the rosary, is recommended. Religious should make an annual spiritual retreat, for which their superiors should give them the necessary means. Last but not least, the daily examination of conscience and the frequent reception

[67] The Latin text uses the subjunctive.

of the sacrament of penance are recommended, in accordance with the provisions of c. 630.

b) Common Life and Lawful Absence (c. 665)

Religious are bound to observe common life in their own house (see c. 665 §1). In particular, this obligation distinguishes a religious from a member of a secular institute. However, there may be legitimate reasons for a religious to be absent for a certain period of time. Three legitimate reasons for absence are recognized by the Code of Canon Law:

- caring for ill health
- studies
- exercising an apostolate in the name of the institute

In addition, there is the lawful absence for military service.[68] An absence for any other reason than those mentioned requires a just cause and is limited to one year. Permission to absent from the religious house may be granted by the major superior, with the consent of his council.[69] Absence for more than one year for any reason other than the three mentioned in the Code may call for an exclaustration, without prejudice to other provisions in the proper law of an institute.

[68] "Decretum de Religiosis servitio militari adstrictis," July 30, 1957, *AAS* 49 (1957): 871–74: "*Sodalis, servitii militaris tempore, legitime a domo religiosa absens est et, proinde, vitae religiosae obligationibus manet obstrictus quae, iuxta Superioris maioris iudicium, cum eius condicione militari componi possunt*" (art. 4 §1).

[69] This also applies to monasteries of cloistered nuns: "The limitation in the Instruction *Verbi Sponsa* has been repealed; for just cause the major superior, according to the norm of can. 665, § 1 CIC, with the consent of her council, may authorize the absence from the monastery of a nun with solemn vows for not more than a year, after hearing the diocesan bishop or the competent religious ordinary" (CO 176).

A religious who is lawfully absent continues to be a member of the institute with all rights and obligations. They remain subject to their lawful superior and must return when the superior recalls them. The decree or (preferably written) agreement by which the superior permits the absence should also regulate the following matters (see GoF 67):

- the contacts that the religious must keep with the institute
- the exercise of rights (active and passive voice, etc.)
- the financial assistance that the superiors may deem necessary to give

The bishop of the place where the religious stays during his absence should be informed. He must be informed if the religious is a cleric. Permission for lawful absence is for a specific reason and for a specific time. If the reason has ceased to exist (e.g., completion of studies) or if the time for which permission was granted has expired, the religious must return. The religious, on the other hand, has the right to return at any time and must be reintegrated into his community.

Besides a lawful absence, there is also an unlawful absence "with the intention of withdrawing from the power of the superior" (c. 665 §2), which may be grounds for dismissal from the institute (see c. 694 §1,3°; c. 696 §1).

Further reading: Teodoro Bahíllo Ruiz, *Los religiosos ausentes de la casa religiosa según el canon 665* (Ediurcla, 1994).

c) Use of Means of Social Communication (c. 666)

The use of means of social communication is addressed in c. 666, whereby the legislator had in mind, in particular, television, radio, and newspapers, and could hardly have imagined the means of social communication available today. In any case, discernment is required when dealing with social communication media. A complete ban is just as inappropriate as excessive use. Depending on the nature of the institute and the activities of individual religious, access to the internet may be essential. A presence on social media platforms is important for pastoral and public relations work. In the novitiate, new members should be instructed in the appropriate use of means of social communication according to the nature of the institute. *Cor Orans* 168–71 calls for the use of means of social communication with sobriety and discretion in monasteries of nuns. The contemplative silence of the monastery should not be undermined. Use for purposes of information, formation, or work may be permitted according to rules to be established by the conventual chapter.

d) Cloister (c. 667)

In order to support a certain separation from the world that is proper to religious institutes (see c. 607 §3) and to protect the privacy of the members, a part of each house is to be reserved for the members alone as a cloister, in accordance with the character and mission of the institute. The nature and extent of the cloister is to be determined by proper law (see c. 667 §1). Monasteries ordered to contemplative life must observe a stricter discipline of cloister (see c. 667 §2). Monasteries of nuns that do not observe the papal cloister, which enables them to engage in apostolic work outside the monastery and to extend hospitality in the monastery, define a cloister adapted to their proper character in the constitutions (see c. 667 §3; CO 204–18). Papal cloister is to be observed by monasteries of nuns that are ordered entirely to contemplative life (see c. 667 §3). This form of cloister is regulated according to the norms given by the Apostolic See (see CO 183–203) and excludes external works of apostolate. The diocesan bishop has the right to enter the cloister of a monastery of nuns in his diocese for a just cause and, with the consent of the major superior, to allow other persons to enter (see c. 667 §4). The dispensation from the cloister for monasteries of nuns rests solely with the major superior, who needs consent of her council if such a dispensation exceeds fifteen days (see CO 175). Neither the diocesan bishop nor the religious ordinary may intervene in granting dispensation from the cloister (see CO 174).[70]

Further reading: Sean O. Sheridan, "To Seek the Face of God: The Cloister and Renewal of Women's Contemplative Monasteries," *Jur* 76 (2016): 415–46.

e) Legal Implications of the Vow of Poverty (c. 668)

The manner in which the evangelical counsel of poverty is to be lived in an institute, according to its nature and purpose, is to be determined in the constitutions (see c. 598 §1). The vow of poverty implies "a dependence and limitation on the use and disposition of goods in accord with the norms of proper law. The juridic emphasis, therefore, is on a poverty of life-style and limitation with respect to material goods."[71] It means a renunciation—in some institutes, even the total renunciation—of the administration of one's own goods.

Before their first profession, candidates are to cede the administration of their goods to whomever they prefer, unless the constitutions provide otherwise. They are to dispose freely of their use and revenue (see c. 668 §1). How this is put into practice depends on the nature of the property. For example, if the property is real estate, the appointment of an administrator is necessary. On the other hand, if the assets are liquid funds, it makes sense to use a form of investment in which the accrued interest is automatically added to the capital. It is up to the candidate to decide who to appoint as asset manager.

[70] This derogation from c. 667 §4 in CO 174–75 was approved by the pope *in forma specifica*.

[71] Sharon A. Euart, "Religious Institutes and the Juridical Relationship of the Members to the Institute," *Jur* 51 (1991): 110.

It can be a family member, the finance officer of the institute or province, or an asset management agency. At least before perpetual profession, a religious is required to make a will that is also valid in civil law (see c. 668 §1). Institutes usually have a model will, while members are free to use their own forms, as long as they are valid in civil law. The religious is free to choose whom they designate as the beneficiary. This can be the institute, but it is not obligatory. In addition, it is highly recommended that a religious draws up a living will in conformity with civil law.[72] In order to change these dispositions for a just cause and in order to place any act concerning temporal goods, a religious needs the permission of the superior competent in accordance with the norms of proper law (see c. 668 §2). Everything that a religious earns through personal effort or by reason of the institute they earn for the institute. Whatever a religious acquires in any way by reason of a pension, subsidy, or insurance, they acquire for the institute, unless proper law provides otherwise (see c. 668 §3). If the latter is the case, proper law should specify in as much detail as possible what a religious acquires for the institute and what they acquire for themself.

A religious who, because of the nature of the institute, must renounce their goods completely, which is usually the case in orders where solemn profession is made, must make this renunciation before perpetual profession in a form that is also valid in civil law, as far as possible (see c. 668 §4). Whether such a renunciation is recognized in civil law depends. In the United States, for example, it is not. The renunciation must be effective from the day of profession. In some institutes, the renunciation is not obligatory, but proper law leaves the decision to the individual religious with the permission of the

[72] For sample forms for an agreement regarding cession of administration, a testament, and a living will, see Miller and Jaramillo, *Procedural Handbook*, 113. It should first be clarified whether these forms are valid under civil law. Consulting an attorney is highly recommended.

supreme moderator. Usually, a certain number of years (typically ten or more) must have elapsed since perpetual profession. A religious who has completely renounced their goods loses the capacity to acquire and possess goods. Therefore, acts contrary to the vow of poverty are invalid.[73] Whatever belongs to the professed after renunciation belongs to the institute according to the norm of proper law (see c. 668 §5).

Further reading: Rosemary Smith, "The Personal Patrimony of Individual Members of Religious Institutes: Current Issues," *CLSA Proceedings* 62 (2000): 263–81; Yuji Sugawara, "La povertà evangelica nel codice: Norma comune (can. 600) e applicazione individuale (can. 668)," *PRC* 89 (2000): 45–77.

f) Religious Habit (c. 669)

The habit (or garb) of an institute is a sign of consecration and a witness of poverty. What the habit is and when it is to be worn is left entirely to the proper law of the institute (see c. 669 §1). There are institutes (e.g., the Society of Jesus) that do not have their own habit. In this case, the clerics of the institute should wear a clerical dress according to the norms of the bishops' conference and the legitimate local customs (see c. 284). The dress of the lay members of the institute is to be determined by proper law (see c. 669 §2).

Further reading: Nancy Bauer, "The Religious Habit in Church Law from 1917 to the Present," *StudCan* 52 (2018): 45–80; Victor G. D'Souza, "Religious Habit and Ecclesiastical Dress: Canon Law and Ecclesial Values," *Indian Theological Studies* 40 (2003): 323–56; Doris Gottemoeller, "Religious Habits Reconsidered," *RfR* 68 (2009): 181–91.

[73] At least according to canon law. In civil law, such acts are not necessarily invalid.

g) Responsibility of the Institute to Care for the Members (c. 670)

As a consequence of the vow of poverty, the institute is obliged to provide its members "with all those things which are necessary to achieve the purpose of their vocation, according to the norm of the constitutions" (c. 670). This very general norm has no parallel in the 1917 Code of Canon Law and no sources in the documents of the Second Vatican Council. The obligation includes but is not limited to material needs. It also includes spiritual care, professional and spiritual formation, and all that serves to maintain mental and physical health, including adequate time for recreation. What is considered necessary varies greatly depending on the nature and purpose of an institute and cannot be generalized. The obligation extends to all members of the institute, including those who are absent (even unlawfully) and exclaustrated.

h) Functions and Offices Outside the Institute (c. 671)

In profession, a religious commits himself entirely to the institute. As a consequence, a religious may not assume functions or offices outside their institute without the permission of the competent superior according to proper law (see c. 671). The norm is broadly defined and is not limited to the acceptance of offices. It also includes any functions outside the institute, such as volunteer work.

i) Further Obligations (c. 672)

All religious, lay as well as clerics, are bound by the prescripts of cc. 277, 285, 286, 287, and 289 from the obligation of clerics. Specifically, this means:

- *celibacy (c. 277):* Celibacy means "perfect and perpetual continence for the sake of the kingdom of heaven" (c. 277 §1). This is a duplication of the obligation of chastity that follows from c. 599.

- *to refrain completely from all things that are unbecoming to their state (c. 285 §§1–2):* Religious are to refrain completely from all things that are unbecoming to their state, and they are to avoid all things that are, though not unbecoming, nevertheless foreign to their state. What this means in detail is determined by proper law and local traditions.

- *prohibition to assume public offices which entail a participation in the exercise of civil power (c. 285 §3):* Religious are forbidden to assume public offices which entail a participation in the exercise of civil power. This includes offices in civil administration and jurisdiction, as well as to be a member of a legislative body. "It would also seem that members of zoning boards, school boards, and similar bodies may participate in the exercise of civil power, and if so these would also be forbidden offices."[74] A dispensation may be granted in justified individual cases.

- *prohibition to take on the management of goods belonging to lay persons or secular offices which entail an obligation of rendering accounts (c. 285 §4):* Religious are prohibited from administering goods belonging to lay people or from holding secular offices that involve the obligation to render accounts without the permission of their ordinary.[75] This includes, for example, serving as power of attorney for an elderly parent or as executor of a relative's estate. Furthermore, religious are forbidden to give surety, even with their own goods, without permission

[74] James H. Provost, "Clergy and Religious in Political Office: Canonical Comments in the American Context," *Jur* 44 (1984): 294.

[75] If according to c. 285 §4 permission required from the ordinary, in lay institutes of pontifical right, this permission can be granted by the major superior, although he is not an ordinary (see c. 672).

of their proper ordinary. Nor are they to sign promissory notes, especially those by which they assume an obligation to pay on demand.

- *business or trade (c. 286):* Religious are forbidden, except with the permission of the competent authority according to proper law, to engage in business or trade for their own benefit or that of others, either personally or through others.
- *political parties and labor unions (c. 287):* Religious may take no active part in political parties or in governing labor unions unless, in the judgment of the competent authority according to proper law, the protection of the rights of the church or the promotion of the common good require it.
- *military service (c. 289 §1):* Religious are not to volunteer for military service except with the permission of their ordinary. In practice, this mainly affects religious who wish to join the armed forces as military chaplains.
- *to use exemptions from exercising functions and public civil offices foreign to their state (c. 289 §2):* Religious are encouraged to make use of the applicable civil exemptions from the exercise of functions and public civil offices foreign to their state. This includes, for example, serving on a jury, if the civil law recognizes their state as an excusing cause. Exceptions may be made in special cases at the discretion of the proper ordinary.

Further reading: Joseph Koonamparampil, "Clerical Obligations Applied to the Religious: An Exegesis of Can. 672," *CpRM* 69 (1988): 111–44 (part 1/3), 271–84 (part 2/3), 365–83 (part 3/3); James H. Provost, "Clergy and Religious in Political Office: Canonical Comments in the American Context," *Jur* 44 (1984): 276–303.

j) Permission to Publish Writings (c. 832)

Not in the chapter of the Code of Canon Law on the rights and obligations of institutes and their members, but in the third book of the Code on the teaching function of the church, in the fourth title, on the instruments of social communication and books, c. 832 contains another obligation of religious: They require the permission of their major superior for the publication of writings dealing with questions of religion or morals,[76] according to the provisions of the constitutions. The competent superior "should not proceed to do so until he has the prior judgment of at least one censor he considers reliable and is satisfied that the work does not contain anything which might be harmful to the doctrine of the faith or morals."[77] If it is a matter of ongoing collaboration in the publication of periodical literature, this permission may be given in a general way.[78]

Further reading: Congregation for the Doctrine of the Faith, *Instruction on Some Aspects of the Use of the Instruments of Social Communication in Promoting the Doctrine of the Faith* (Pauline, 1992); also available at https://www.vatican.va/roman_curia/congregations/cfaith/documents/rc_con_cfaith_doc_19920330_istruzione-pccs_en.html.

[76] The provisions of c. 832 apply only to writings dealing with matters of religion or morals. It does not apply, for example, to writings dealing with art, history, literature, science, and so on.

[77] Congregation for the Doctrine of the Faith, *Instruction on Some Aspects of the Use of the Instruments of Social Communication in Promoting the Doctrine of the Faith*, (Pauline, 1992), no. IV, 17 §1. Also available at https://www.vatican.va/roman_curia/congregations/cfaith/documents/rc_con_cfaith_doc_19920330_istruzione-pccs_en.html.

[78] See Congregation for the Doctrine of the Faith, *Instruction on Some Aspects*, no. IV, 17 §3.

5. Apostolate of Institutes (cc. 673–683)

The apostolate that all institutes have in common "consists first of all in the witness of their consecrated life, which they are bound to foster by prayer and penance" (c. 673) according to their own patrimony. An institute also has one of the following apostolates, depending on the nature and purpose of the institute:

- *institutes that are entirely ordered to contemplation (c. 674):* Institutes that are entirely contemplative do not engage in external apostolic activity. They "hold a distinguished place in the mystical Body of Christ" and through their life of contemplation "extend it with hidden apostolic fruitfulness" (c. 674). The members of these institutes cannot be called to assist in pastoral ministries, however much the needs of the active apostolate may require it. The Carthusians, for example, belong to this category.
- *institutes dedicated to works of the apostolate (c. 675):* These include institutes whose purpose is external apostolic activity (e.g., the Society of Jesus), as well as contemplative institutes that combine their contemplative life with active apostolic work (e.g., Benedictines). The whole life of the members of those institutes is to be imbued with an apostolic spirit, and the apostolic spirit shall be imbued by religious spirit according to the patrimony of the institute. Their apostolic work is exercised in the name and by the mandate of the church and therefore is to be carried out in the communion with the church.
- *lay institutes (c. 676):* The apostolate of lay institutes, both male and female, consists in spiritual and corporal works of mercy through which they participate in the pastoral mission of the church.

Superiors and members are to faithfully maintain the apostolate proper to the institute. Attentive to the needs of the times and places, they should prudently accommodate them, even by the use of new and appropriate means (see c. 677 §1). Third orders (the name varies according to the institute) are associations of the faithful whose members share the spirit of a religious institute in their secular life (see c. 303). Institutes are to take special care of them so that they may be imbued with the proper spirit of the institute (see c. 677 §2).

The coordination of the entire apostolate in a diocese is in the hands of the diocesan bishop (see c. 680). Regarding religious institutes, he must take into account the characteristics and purposes of each institute and the intentions of its founders. More detailed principles, guidelines, and norms on this can be found in *Mutuae Relationes*, which offers the directives of the Congregation for Bishops and the Congregation for Religious of May 14, 1978, regarding the relations between bishops and religious. Although these directives were issued before the 1983 Code of Canon Law came into force, they are still applicable. At this writing, they are being revised. For the care of souls, public worship, and other works of the apostolate, a religious is subject to the diocesan bishop (see c. 678 §1). In these areas, the bishop is the ecclesiastical superior of the religious, and the religious is subject to the authority and direction of the bishop (see c. 681 §1), though the bishop is not the hierarchical superior. The vow of obedience does not bind the religious in relation to the bishop. The hierarchical superior remains the superior within the institute. A religious must also observe the discipline of the institute with regard to apostolic activity (see c. 678 §2). This makes it necessary for the bishop and the superior to be in constant dialogue regarding the apostolic activity of a religious (see c. 678 §3). It is advisable for the bishop and the competent superior to draw up a written agreement, also including financial matters (see c. 681 §2).[79] When a religious is to be assigned to an eccle-

[79] A sample agreement can be found in Miller and Jaramillo, *Procedural Handbook*, 206.

siastical office, the diocesan bishop appoints him on the presentation of the competent superior or at least with his consent (see c. 682 §1). Both the diocesan bishop and the superior can freely remove a religious from office by means of a written decree addressed to the religious concerned (see c. 193 §3–4), after having informed the other (see c. 682 §2). There is no right to be heard or to give consent; mere notification is sufficient. Other provisions for removal from office do not apply in this case.[80] The religious has the right of appeal against their removal. The fact that the removal can be carried out freely by the bishop or superior does not mean that it can be arbitrary. Although a right of appeal is not explicitly mentioned in c. 682 §2, it is given because a violation of the religious's rights is possible.

The diocesan bishop has the right but not the obligation to visit churches and oratories habitually attended by the faithful, schools (see c. 806 §1), and other works of religion or charity entrusted to religious, with the exception of schools open exclusively to the institute's own students, either personally or through a delegate (see c. 683 §1). If the diocesan bishop discovers abuses during the visitation, he must first report them to the superior of the institute. If the superior does not take action, the diocesan bishop may himself take precautionary measures (see c. 683 §2).

A diocesan bishop can coerce a religious with penalties in all matters in that the religious is subject to him (see c. 1320). In addition, a diocesan bishop can prohibit a religious from residing in his diocese for a most grave reason, if he has informed the religious's superior and the latter has failed to make the necessary provisions (see c. 679). The matter must be brought to the attention of the Apostolic See.

[80] For example, cc. 1740–1747 on the removal of a pastor do not apply in the case of a religious.

Further reading: James J. Conn, "Bishops and the Apostolates of Religious," *CLSA Proceedings* 57 (1995): 49–83; Joseph A. Galante, "The Relationship of the Diocesan Bishop and Institutes of Pontifical Right," *CLSA Proceedings* 57 (1995): 90–96; Joanne Graham, "The Relation between Religious Institutes and the Diocese," *CLSA Proceedings* 60 (1998): 82–90; Richard A. Hill, "An Overview of *Mutuae Relationes*," in *Code, Community, Ministry: Selected Studies for the Parish Minister Introducing the Revised Code of Canon Law*, ed. James H. Provost (Canon Law Society of America, 1983), 81–85; Sharon L. Holland, "Bishop and Religious: Right Relationship for Ecclesial Mission," *CLSA Proceedings* 73 (2011): 108–17; Rose McDermott, "Associates and Associations Joined to Religious Institutes," *CLSA Proceedings* 60 (1998): 132–49; Rose McDermott, "Ecclesiastical Authority and Religious Autonomy: Canon 679 under Glass," *StudCan* 38 (2004): 461–80; Antony Pinheiro, "Bishops-Religious Relationship (can. 678, §§ 1–2)," *CpRM* 68 (1987): 35–76.

6. Separation from the Institute (cc. 684–704)

By profession, a religious is bound to a community, in the case of regular canons and monks even to the community of a particular house. However, there may be various reasons that make separation from the community necessary. The increasing number of closures of houses, provinces, and even entire institutes can confront a religious with the question of transfer or departure, even through no fault of their own. On February 2, 2020, the Congregation for Institutes of Consecrated Life and Societies of Apostolic Life published guidelines entitled *The Gift of Fidelity, The Joy of Perseverance*,[81] which provide a very useful compilation of the juridical norms concerning separation from the institute. It should be noted, how-

[81] See n. 64 above.

ever, that the norms regarding separation from the institute have been modified several times since the publication of the guidelines. The Code of Canon Law distinguishes four forms of separation of a religious from the institute: transfer, exclaustration, departure, and dismissal.[82]

Further reading: Congregation for Institutes of Consecrated Life and Societies of Apostolic Life, *The Gift of Fidelity, The Joy of Perseverance* (Libreria Editrice Vaticana, 2020); Daniel Tibi, " 'The Gift of Fidelity, the Joy of Perseverance.' Separation from Religious Institutes According to the Latest Roman Documents," *RfR* 3 (2023): 47–61.

a) Transfer (cc. 684–685)

The Code of Canon Law distinguishes three types of transfer:

- transfer from one institute to another,
- transfer from one autonomous monastery to another of the same institute or of the same federation or of the same confederation, and
- transfer to or from a secular institute or a society of apostolic life.

A transfer of any kind can be requested only by the religious concerned and cannot be imposed by the institute, without prejudice to any provisions in the proper law that may provide for a temporary transfer.

[82] See Miller and Jaramillo, *Procedural Handbook*, 153–85, for useful instructions on the procedure for the various types of separation from the institute, including sample forms. It should be noted, however, that the norms on separation from the institute have been modified since the publication of the book. Some procedures therefore need to be adapted to the new procedural norms.

Further reading: Rosmin Cheruvilparambil, "Transfer between Religious Institutions: Requirements, Process and Effects," *Iustitia: Dharmaram Journal of Canon Law* 11 (2020): 187–201.

aa) Transfer from One Institute to Another Institute (c. 684 §§1–2)

Transfer from one institute to another is possible only for religious with perpetual vows. Religious with temporary vows who wish to change institutes must first lawfully leave their own institute (by expiry of the period for which the vows were taken or by indult of departure) and undergo a new novitiate in the new institute.

For a transfer from one institute to another, a religious needs the consent of the supreme moderator of each institute and their respective councils. The duration of the probationary time is least three years (see c. 684 §2). The proper law of the new institute determines the manner of the probation, whereas the probationary period is not a new novitiate. During the probationary period, the rights and obligations in the original institute are suspended with the vows remaining, and the religious is bound to observe the proper law of the new institute (see c. 685 §1). If, after the probationary period in the new institute, the religious does not make profession or is not admitted to profession in the new institute, they must return to their original institute. If, on the other hand, they wish to make profession in the new institute and are admitted according to proper law, the religious is incorporated into the new institute while the vows, rights, and obligations in the original institute cease (see c. 685 §2). The new institute should officially inform the original institute about the transfer. If the religious is a cleric, he is incardinated in the new institute after his profession (see c. 266 §2; c. 268 §2).

bb) Transfer from One Autonomous Monastery to Another of the Same Institute, Federation, or Confederation (c. 684 §§3–4)

A transfer from one autonomous monastery (e.g., Benedictine abbey) to another of the same institute, federation, or confederation is similarly possible for religious in perpetual vows as well as for religious in temporary vows.[83] In this case, the consent of the major superior of each monastery and of the chapter of the receiving monastery is required and sufficient (see c. 684 §3), without prejudice to any further requirements that may arise from proper law. A new profession is not necessary. The manner and duration of the probationary period in the new institute is determined by its proper law (see c. 684 §4). If the religious wishes to remain in the new monastery after the probationary period and is accepted by it according to the provisions of the proper law, the major superior must issue a decree of the transfer. The new monastery shall inform the original monastery of the transfer.

cc) Transfer to or from a Secular Institute or a Society of Apostolic Life (c. 684 §5)

If it concerns a transfer to or from a secular institute or a society of apostolic life, the matter must be submitted to the Apostolic See, whose mandates must be observed (see c. 684 §5).

b) Exclaustration (cc. 686–687)

Exclaustration means "the absence from common life of a perpetual professed member who, while remaining a member of the institute, is authorized by the competent Superior to reside outside the community" (GoF 70). Exclaustration can be requested by the member, or it can be imposed by the competent authority.

[83] See the authentic interpretation of c. 684 §3 of June 20, 1987: *AAS* 79 (1987): 1249.

aa) Exclaustration Requested by the Member (c. 686 §§1–2)

Exclaustration can only be requested by a religious in perpetual vows for a grave cause (e.g., discernment of one's vocation) after a written request. It is often, but not necessarily, the first step toward permanent separation from the institute. Exclaustration for a member in temporal vows is not possible.

Exclaustration for religious men and for religious women who are not nuns may be granted by the supreme moderator of the institute, with the consent of their council, not exceeding five years.[84] It is up to the proper law of an institute to determine whether this five-year term is intended to be continuous or not. According to the administrative practice of the Dicastery for Institutes of Consecrated Life and Societies of Apostolic Life, the supreme moderator has the possibility of granting an indult for a new five-year term, when at least five years have passed since the previous expiration of the indult. If the religious requesting exclaustration is a cleric, the ordinary of the place where the religious will reside during the period of exclaustration must consent. If the religious is not a cleric, the local ordinary should at least be informed. To grant an exclaustration of more than five years, the Apostolic See is competent in the case of institutes of pontifical right or the diocesan bishop in the case of institutes of diocesan right (see c. 686 §1).

To grant an indult of exclaustration for nuns (of a monastery of pontifical right as well as of a monastery of diocesan right) is generally reserved to the Apostolic See (see c. 686 §2), but exceptions were introduced by *Cor Orans*. An indult of exclaustration for a period of up to one year may be issued by the major superior (e.g., abbess or prioress) with the consent

[84] The period for which the supreme moderator with consent of their council may grant exclaustration was increased from three to five years in the apostolic letter *Competentias Quasdam* (2022).

of her council, after approval by the ordinary of the place where the nun will reside and consultation with the diocesan bishop in the case of institutes of diocesan right, or with the competent supreme moderator (e.g., general superior or abbot president) in the case of institutes of pontifical right (see CO 177). Beyond this one year, the president of the federation to which the monastery belongs may, with the consent of the federation council, extend the indult of exclaustration for a maximum of two years. For this purpose, a written opinion of the major superior of the nun in question, collegial with her council, is required, given after obtaining the consent of the ordinary of the place where the exclaustrated nun will reside and obtaining an opinion of the diocesan bishop in the case of institutes of diocesan right or of the competent supreme moderator in the case of institutes of pontifical right (see CO 130; 178–179). An indult of exclaustration for nuns of more than three years can only be granted by the Apostolic See. For this purpose, the request of the nun concerned, as well as the consent of the president of the federation and of the federation council, are submitted to the Apostolic See. Before the consent is given, the written opinion of the major superior, collegially with her council, is required, which is given after the consent of the ordinary of the place where the exclaustrated nun will reside and the approving opinion of the diocesan bishop in the case of institutes of diocesan right or of the competent supreme moderator in the case of institutes of pontifical right (see CO 131; 180).

A special form of exclaustration, which is not mentioned in the Code of Canon Law but arises from the administrative practice of the Apostolic See, is the *exclaustratio qualificata* (qualified exclaustration). It can only be granted by the Apostolic See at the written request of the religious concerned. It addresses religious priests who have doubts about their vocation and who, in order to clarify their situation, wish to live for some time in the world like lay people. The indult of exclaustration is usually granted for one or two years. It includes the prohibition of wearing the habit of the institute or other clerical garb, the prohibition of the exercise of ordination and of any activity as a priest, and the suspension of any rights and obligations arising from the vows, with the exception of the obligation of chastity.

bb) Imposed Exclaustration (c. 686 §3)

Exclaustration may not only be requested by the religious themself but may also be imposed on them for grave reasons. This shall primarily protect the community if the religious in question seriously impairs community life or common work. The Apostolic See, in the case of institutes of pontifical right, or the diocesan bishop, in the case of institutes of diocesan right, at the request of the supreme moderator with the consent of their council, is competent to grant the imposed exclaustration. Before making the request, the supreme moderator shall inform the religious concerned, give them the reasons, and allow them the opportunity to defend themself (see c. 50). The duration of the imposed exclaustration, the place of residence of the exclaustrated religious, and other provisions are determined by the competent ecclesiastical authority in the decree of exclaustration. The major superior shall notify in writing the bishop of the place where the exclaustrated religious will reside.

cc) Rights and Obligations Arising from Exclaustration (c. 687)

The legal position of an exclaustrated religious is the same in case of requested exclaustration and in case of imposed exclaustration. The exclaustrated religious remains a member of the institute, and they remain under the care of their competent superiors, and, if they are a cleric, also under the care of the local ordinary. They lack active and passive voice, and they are considered freed from the obligations that cannot be reconciled with the new condition of their life. They can wear the habit of the institute unless the indult of exclaustration determines otherwise. Further provisions (e.g., obligation to reside in a certain place) can be made in the decree. The financial aspect should not be ignored either. Since the exclaustrated religious continues to be a member of the institute, the institute continues to have the obligation to care for them, not only pastorally but also financially (see c. 670). As far as possible, it seems appropriate that the exclaustrated religious provides for their own personal needs and earns their own living. If this is not possible (e.g., because of old age, illness, or unemployment), the institute must support them financially.[85] Agreements concerning financial matters should be made in writing between the institute and the exclaustrated religious.

Further reading: Mayong Andreas Acin, "The Exclaustration of Religious. Law and Praxis," *StudCan* 56 (2022): 299–321; Patrick Cogan, "Exclaustration and Social Security and Pension Benefits," *RRAO* 2006: 56–57; William A. Schumacher and J. James Cuneo, "Exclaustration," *RRAO* 1985: 20–23; Patrick T. Shea, "Exclaustration," *CLSA Proceedings* 59 (1997): 267–81.

c) Departure (cc. 688–693)

Departure is the definite separation from the institute at the initiative of the religious.

aa) Departure of a Religious in Temporary Vows (cc. 688–689)

A religious in temporary vows can depart from their institute when the time of their temporary profession has been completed (see c. 688 §1). In this case, no further formalities are required for departure. If a religious in temporary vows

[85] Regarding social security and pension, see Patrick Cogan, "Exclaustration and Social Security and Pension Benefits," *RRAO* 2006: 56–57.

wishes to leave the institute before the completion of their temporary profession for a grave reason, they can obtain an indult of departure from the supreme moderator with the consent of their council (see c. 688 §2). This applies to institutes of pontifical right as well as to institutes of diocesan right.[86] Only in the case of autonomous monasteries, according to c. 615, the indult of departure needs the confirmation of the diocesan bishop to be valid.

When the period of temporary profession has expired, it may also be that the religious in question applies for admission to further profession (be it admission to a further temporary profession or be it admission to perpetual profession), but the competent superior does not want to admit them to the subsequent profession (see c. 689 §1). In this case, the competent major superior, after having heard the council, can for a just cause exclude a religious from making a subsequent profession when the period of temporary profession has been elapsed (see c. 689 §1).[87] A just cause may be that the religious is unable[88] or unwilling to live the observance of the institute, or that they do not integrate themself into the community. Physical or mental illness that, in the opinion of experts,[89] renders a religious unfit to lead the life of the institute, constitutes a just cause for not admitting to renewal of profession or to perpetual profession, unless the illness was contracted through the negligence of the institute or through work performed in the institute (see c. 689 §2). If a religious becomes insane[90] during

[86] This regulation was extended to institutes of diocesan right through the apostolic letter *Competentias Quasdam*. Formerly, for institutes of diocesan right, the confirmation of the diocesan bishop was required for the validity of the indult.

[87] See Opondo, *Temporary Profession and Exclusion*.

[88] Life as a Carthusian monk, for example, is physically and mentally demanding. It may be that a candidate is simply not capable of meeting these demands.

[89] See n. 64 above.

[90] See n. 65 above.

temporary profession, they cannot be dismissed from the institute, even if they are incapable of subsequent profession (see c. 689 §3). In practice, however, it will be difficult to distinguish between becoming mentally ill and becoming insane. These could be cases where someone is unable to make a decision for or against profession for psychological reasons. Such a religious would be suspended in the state of temporary profession and would have to receive the necessary treatment until they are able again to make a decision. Non-admission to subsequent profession is to be made by written decree of the competent superior, which must at least give a summary of the reasons (see c. 51). An administrative recourse against the non-admission is possible.

bb) Departure of a Religious in Perpetual Vows (cc. 691–693)

A religious in perpetual vows may request an indult of departure for the gravest of causes considered before God (see c. 691 §1). A religious should, in this case, seek the help and advice of prudent and experienced persons (see GoF 78). The authority responsible for granting an indult of departure is in all cases an authority outside the institute: in the case of institutes of pontifical right, the Apostolic See, and in the case of institutes of diocesan right, the bishop of the diocese to which the religious in question belongs, although in this case, too, the Apostolic See may be approached (see c. 691 §2). If a religious intends to request an indult of departure, they shall submit the written request to the supreme moderator of the institute. The latter forwards the request, together with their opinion and the opinion of their council, to the competent authority. Since it is important to obtain close information in order to judge the matter adequately, the competent major superior (e.g., abbot or prior of an autonomous house or major superior of a province) should also give an opinion, since they usually know the religious in question better than the supreme moderator, especially in the case of international institutes. In giving their opinion, the superiors shall consider the validity and gravity of the reasons, having in mind both the good of the religious concerned and the good of the institute. If the indult of departure is granted according to the request, the religious must be notified (see c. 692). The religious requesting the indult may withdraw their request at any time during the procedure, and they have the right to reject the decree in the act of notification. The indult of departure comes into force if the religious is notified and does not reject it. The notification is usually made in writing with acknowledgment of receipt (see c. 56). The indult may also be read to the religious in the presence of a notary or two witnesses (see c. 55). In this case, a record of what has occurred must be prepared, and all those present must sign it. The indult of departure lawfully notified and not rejected entails by the law itself dispensation from the vows and from all the obligations arising from profession (see c. 692). One who departs from a religious institute cannot request anything from the institute for any work done in it, though the institute is to observe equity and the charity of the Gospel toward separated religious (see c. 702).

If the religious requesting an indult of departure is a cleric, the indult will be granted only if he has found a bishop willing to incardinate him in his diocese, or at least to receive him experimentally, or if he also requests laicization along with the indult of departure (see c. 693). A letter of intent from the bishop must be attached to the request. In the administrative practice of the Apostolic See, in the case of a cleric, the bishop is given a time limit by which the incardination must have taken place. If the religious is incardinated in the diocese before the expiration of the time limit by decree of the bishop, or by law after the expiration of five years (see c. 693), he legally departs from the institute. If, on the other hand, the bishop rejects him, the procedure must be gone through again, since the Apostolic See always grants an indult of departure for clerics only for a particular diocese.

cc) Readmission after Departure (c. 690)

A religious who has legitimately left the institute after completing the novitiate or after profession[91] can be readmitted in the institute by the supreme moderator with the consent of their council without the obligation to undergo a new novitiate (see c. 690 §1). The supreme moderator shall determine an appropriate period of probation preceding the taking of the temporary vows as well as the duration for which the temporary vows shall be taken. The superior of an autonomous monastery (e.g., the abbot of a Benedictine abbey) with the consent of their council has the same faculty (see c. 690 §2).[92]

Further reading: Evaldo X. Gomes, "Readmissão de candidatos à vida religiosa segundo o cânone 690 do Código de Direito Canônico," *Direito e pastoral* 17 (2003): 45–53; Francis J. Marini, "Readmission of Former Member of Religious Institute," *RRAO* 2006: 174–76.

d) Dismissal (cc. 694–703)

Dismissal is the definitive separation from the institute that is not initiated by the concerned religious themself. A separation from the institute can be a dismissal ipso facto, which occurs by the law itself, or a dismissal by dismissal procedure, which can be mandatory or facultative.

Further reading: Navya Thattil, "Distinctive Motives for Dismissal of Religious in CIC and CCEO," *Iustitia: Dharmaram Journal of Canon Law* 5 (2014): 205–24.

[91] This procedure of readmission does not apply to dismissed members.

[92] This provision applies only to those who wish to reenter and who have completed the novitiate in the same house or who have lawfully left the same house after making their profession. Readmission without the obligation of novitiate in another house of the same congregation or confederation is possible in accordance with the provisions of proper law. In this case, however, a dispensation from the competent authority is required.

aa) Dismissal ipso facto (c. 694)

Dismissal ipso facto occurs by the very fact of having committed the respective violation of an obligation of consecrated life. In this case, there is no dismissal procedure, and no decree of dismissal is issued. The competent superior with their council has to gather the evidence, and the superior issues the statement of the case so that the dismissal is established juridically. The Code of Canon Law lists three grounds for dismissal ipso facto (see c. 694 §1):

- notorious defection from the Catholic faith (c. 694 §1,1°)
- marriage or attempt to marriage, even only civilly (c. 694 §1,2°)
- unlawful absence from the religious house lasting at least twelve consecutive months, if the religious turns out to be untraceable (c. 694 §1,3°)

Anyone who has notoriously defected from the Catholic faith can no longer be a member of a Catholic religious institute. This includes apostasy (the rejection of the Christian faith as a whole), heresy (the denial of a truth of faith), and schism (the refusal to submit under the pope or to stay in communion with the hierarchy of the church). The formal act of leaving the church before a state authority, where this is possible, is also considered a defection from the Catholic faith. Defection from the Catholic faith is notorious when "the fact is disclosed in such a way that it becomes public knowledge, by reason of the means used (press, web, public declaration), or publication of the fact" (GoF 82). In any case, the defection from the Catholic faith must be certain and manifest outwardly. A doubt of faith does not fall under this norm, nor does a purely internal defection from the faith, which is not publicly declared.

Someone cannot live a celibate life and be married at the same time. Therefore, a religious who enters into or tries to enter into a marriage, even a civil marriage, is dismissed ipso facto from the institute. In addition, there are canonical penalties that affect both the religious in question and the person with whom they have contracted or attempted to contract marriage (see c. 1329 §2). If the religious is a cleric, he incurs the penalty of suspension and may be punished by dismissal from the clerical state (see c. 1394 §1). If the religious is not a cleric, they incur the penalty of interdict (see c. 1394 §2). In addition, there is the irregularity for the reception of an ordination (see c. 1041,3°) or for the exercise of an ordination already received (see c. 1044 §1,3°).

The Code provides for dismissal by means of dismissal procedure in the case of an unlawful absence of half a year. However, the religious in question must be notified of the decree of dismissal in order for it to come into force. If the religious is untraceable, this causes serious difficulties. As a solution to this problem, the Code provides the dismissal ipso facto in case of an unlawful absence from the religious house lasting at least twelve consecutive months, if the religious is untraceable. Two facts must be fulfilled: unlawful absence for twelve consecutive months and untraceability. If a religious is unlawfully absent, their superiors are required to seek them out and to help them to return and to persevere in their vocation (see c. 665 §2). If the superiors' attempt to seek out the unlawfully absent religious fails because they are considered untraceable,[93] they evaluate the case with their council and issue a declaration of inability to be contacted (see GoF 86). The twelve-month period begins to run from the date of this declaration. If the religious remains unlawfully absent and untraceable for at least twelve consecutive months—the

[93] On the question of when a religious is considered untraceable, GoF 84 states: "The person whose home address or at least place of residence is known is considered to be available; as is the person who has communicated his or her address/place of residence. A person is to be considered unable to be contacted if one knows only: a telephone number; an e-mail address; a profile on social networks; a fictitious address." A decree of dismissal is normally notified in writing, so a postal address is required.

superior having repeatedly tried to find them or it being generally acknowledged that they deliberately make themself untraceable—dismissal occurs ipso facto. Only in this case the Code prescribes that the statement of the fact of the dismissal ipso facto must be confirmed by an authority external to the institute: in the case of institutes of pontifical right, by the Apostolic See, and in the case of institutes of diocesan right, by the bishop of the principal seat.

Further reading: Congregation for Institutes of Consecrated Life and Societies of Apostolic Life, "Circular Letter on the Motu Proprio of Pope Francis *Communis Vita*," *RRAO* 2020: 24–27; Victor G. D'Souza, "Automatic Dismissal of the Religious from the Religious Institute on the Ground of Marriage," *Studies in Church Law* 6 (2010): 445–52; John Chrysostom Kozlowski, "When an Illegitimate Absence Irreparably Damages Communion: An Analysis of the Motu Proprio *Communis Vita*," *Angelicum* 99 (2022): 231–51; Anthony Malone, "Commentary on Pope Francis' Motu Proprio *Communis Vita*," *The Canonist* 10 (2019): 12–15.

bb) Dismissal through Dismissal Procedure (cc. 695–700)

In addition to dismissal ipso facto, the Code contains norms for dismissal through dismissal procedure, which can be mandatory or facultative.

A religious must be dismissed for the following delicts (see c. 695 §1):

- concubinage (c. 1395 §1)
- other sexual offenses (c. 1395 §2)
- sexual offenses committed by force or by threats or by abuse of authority (c. 1395 §3)
- murder, kidnapping, mutilation, grave wounding of a person (c. 1397 §1)
- abortion (c. 1397 §2)

- sexual offense with a minor or a person whose use of reason is habitually impaired (c. 1398 §1,1°)
- child pornography (c. 1398 §1,2–3°)

In the case of the delicts mentioned in c. 1395 §§2–3 and c. 1398 §1,[94] the major superior may decide that dismissal is not necessary and that correction of the member, restitution of justice, and reparation of scandal can be resolved sufficiently in another way (see c. 695 §2), without prejudice to any canonical penalties according to c. 1398 §1 for clerics and according to c. 1398 §2 for religious who are not clerics. These are cases of a conditionally mandatory dismissal.

It is up to the major superior (their council does not necessarily need to be involved, unlike in the case of a discretionary dismissal) to collect the evidence of the offense and its imputability. The accusation, together with the evidence, must be made known to the religious concerned and they must be given the opportunity to defend themself (see c. 50). The files must be signed by the major superior and a notary and must be sent to the supreme moderator of the institute together with the defenses of the religious concerned (see c. 695 §2). The further course of the proceedings is the same as in the case of a facultative dismissal.

A religious may also be dismissed for reasons other those than mentioned above. It is required that the reasons are serious, external, attributable, and legally proven (see c. 696 §1). The Code lists as possible reasons:

- habitual neglect of the obligations of consecrated life,
- repeated violations of the sacred bonds,
- stubborn disobedience to the legitimate prescripts of superiors in a grave matter,

[94] This faculty has been extended to the delicts mentioned in c. 1398 §1 through the apostolic letter *Recognitum Librum VI* (2022).

- grave scandal arising from the culpable behavior of the member,
- stubborn upholding or diffusion of doctrines condemned by the magisterium of the church,
- public adherence to ideologies of materialism or atheism, and
- illegitimate absence lasting six months.

The list is not complete. Other reasons of the same severity are also eligible. In the case of a religious in temporal vows, they may be less severe (see c. 696 §2).

If the major superior, after having heard their council, decides to begin the process of dismissal, they must first gather all the evidence. Thereafter, the major superior must warn the religious concerned in writing or before two witnesses, with the express threat of dismissal[95] if they do not reform. Thereby, they must clearly state the reason for the threatened dismissal, and they must give the religious the opportunity to defend themself. If the first canonical warning is unsuccessful, the major superior must issue another warning no earlier than fifteen days later. If the second canonical warning is also unsuccessful and the major superior, together with their council, conclude that the religious is incorrigible and that the defenses presented are insufficient, they hand over the files signed by the major superior and a notary, together with the defenses of the religious, to the supreme moderator (see c. 697). From this point of the procedure, the further course is identical to the procedure in case of a mandatory dismissal.

The supreme moderator acts collegially with their council, which must consist of at least four members for validity. They

[95] In practice, there is a risk here of forgetting the threat of dismissal. In that case, a decree of dismissal issued later could be declared invalid due to formal errors.

examine the proofs, the arguments, and the defenses. They then proceed to a secret ballot. If the simple majority votes in favor, the supreme moderator must issue the decree of dismissal, whereby for its validity the reasons in law and in fact must be expressed at least summarily (see c. 699 §1). This procedure is the same both in institutes of pontifical right and in institutes of diocesan right. In autonomous monasteries mentioned in c. 615, the major superior takes the place of the supreme moderator and decides collegially with their council on the dismissal in the manner described above (see c. 699 §2).[96] Confirmation of the decree of dismissal by the Holy See in the case of institutes of pontifical right, or by the diocesan bishop in the case of institutes of diocesan right, is no longer required.[97] The decree of dismissal comes into force when it is made known to the religious in question. The notification is to be made by registered mail with acknowledgment of receipt or personally in the presence of two witnesses. To be valid, the decree must indicate the right to make recourse to the competent authority (that is, the Dicastery for Institutes of Consecrated Life and Societies of Apostolic Life in the case of institutes of pontifical right or the diocesan bishop in the case of institutes of diocesan right) within thirty days from receiving the notification, without the need to request in writing the revocation of the decree from its author (see c. 1734 §1).[98] A recourse has suspensive effect (see c. 700).

[96] This faculty was given to the major superior through the apostolic letter *Competentias Quasdam*. Formerly, in this case, the competent diocesan bishop was the one to decide on the dismissal.

[97] The confirmation by an external authority was abolished through the apostolic letter *Competentias Quasdam*. The rights of the dismissed religious are considered sufficiently protected through the right to make recourse to the competent authority.

[98] The time limit for recourse was increased from ten to thirty days through the apostolic letter *Expedit ut Iura* (2023).

cc) Legal Effects of Dismissal (cc. 701–702)

By lawful dismissal, vows as well as rights and obligations deriving from profession cease. If the dismissed religious is a cleric, he cannot exercise sacred orders until he finds a bishop who receives him into the diocese (see c. 693) or at least permits him to exercise sacred orders (see c. 701). Since a dismissed cleric is no longer incorporated into the institute, incardination thereby ceases. This results in the particularity of a cleric without incardination, which is explicitly rejected in c. 265.

One who has been dismissed from a religious institute cannot request anything from the institute for any work done in it, though the institute is to observe equity and the charity of the Gospel toward separated religious (see c. 702).[99]

dd) Immediate Expulsion from a Religious House (c. 703)

A religious may be expelled from a house immediately by the major superior or, if there is danger of delay, by the local superior, with the consent of the council, in case of grave external scandal or grave imminent harm to the institute. This is a precautionary measure to avert possible harm to the community. It is sufficient that the scandal or harm be due to the religious in question. He need not necessarily be guilty. The case is to be referred to the Apostolic See for further instruction. Alternatively, the procedure of dismissal may be initiated.

e) Report of Separations to the Apostolic See (c. 704)

All members separated in any way from the institute must be mentioned in the periodic report to the Apostolic See prescribed by c. 592 §1.

[99] For further details, see Rose McDermott, "Canon 702, § 2: Equity and Charity to Separated Members," *CLSA Proceedings* 52 (1990): 120–33.

7. Religious Raised to the Episcopate (cc. 705–707)

The special case of a religious becoming a bishop is dealt with in cc. 705–707. These norms apply equally to the appointment as diocesan bishop and as auxiliary bishop. In analogous application of c. 431 of the Code of Canons of the Eastern Churches and due to the fact that these cases are also mentioned in c. 706,1°, it can be assumed that cc. 705–707 also apply to religious in an office equivalent in law to a diocesan bishop but without having received episcopal ordination (see c. 381 §2).

A religious raised to the episcopate remains a member of his institute. By virtue of the vow of obedience, he is subject only to the pope and no longer to the superiors and chapters of his institute. He is not bound by obligations that, in his own prudent judgment, are incompatible with his state (see c. 705).[100]

With regard to the vow of poverty, a distinction is made as to whether the religious appointed to the office of bishop has completely renounced his goods in his profession or whether he has only ceded the administration of his goods. In the first case, he is entitled to the use, revenue, and administration of the goods that accrue to him, but the property belongs to the particular church which he serves, if it is a diocesan bishop or a person equal in law to him according to c. 381 §2. In the case of an auxiliary bishop, the property belongs to the institute if it has the legal capacity to hold possessions. If the institute is not, the property reverts to the Apostolic See (see c. 706,1°).

[100] According to the authentic interpretation of the Pontifical Commission for Authentic Interpretation of the Code of Canon Law of May 23, 1988, *AAS* 80 (1988): 1818–19, a religious who has been appointed auditor of the Roman Rota is exempt only from those obligations arising from his profession that relate to the exercise of his actual ministry: "*D. Utrum religiosi, Romanae Rotae Praelati Auditores nominati, exempti habendi sint ab Ordinario religioso et ab obligationibus, quae e professione religiosa promanant, ad instar religiosorum ad Episcopatum evectorum. R. Negative ad utrumque, salvis iis quae ad exercitium proprii officii spectant.*"

If the religious appointed to the office of bishop has ceded only the administration of his possessions in his profession, he regains the administration of his possessions previously acquired and acquires ownership of the possessions that belong to him after his appointment as bishop (see c. 706,2°). In any case, the intention of the donor is to be respected with regard to all goods that do not belong to him personally (see c. 706,3°). For example, with regard to donations, it is necessary to distinguish whether they are for the personal use of the bishop or for the diocese or for the institute.

The Code of Canon Law makes no statement whether a religious appointed to the office of bishop continues to have active and passive voice in his institute. According to c. 629 §2 of the 1917 Code, he did not. This lacuna in the law has been filled by an authentic interpretation of the Pontifical Commission for Authentic Interpretation of the Code of Canon Law of May 17, 1986, which clarified that a religious appointed to the office of bishop has no active or passive voice in his institute.[101]

A religious who is a retired bishop is free to choose his place of residence, even outside a house of his institute, unless otherwise provided by the Apostolic See (see c. 707 §1). It is up to the wise judgment of the religious to assume if he will be able to reintegrate himself into the community of a house of his institute. It also applies to a religious who is a retired bishop that the bishops' conference must provide for his sufficient and worthy support, with the diocese in which he served being primarily responsible, if the institute itself does not provide for his support (see c. 707 §2; c. 402 §2). If the religious was not a bishop in the service of a diocese, but, for example, in the service of a dicastery of the Apostolic See, the Apostolic See must provide for his support after retirement (c. 707 §2).

[101] *AAS* 78 (1986): 1323–1324: "*D. Utrum Episcopus religiosus gaudeat in proprio instituto voce activa et passiva. R. Negative.*"

Further reading: Arul Kumar Sebastian, *Religious Elevated to Episcopate: A Historical, Theological and Juridical Approach in CIC/1983* (Pontificia Università Gregoriana, 2022).

8. Conferences of Major Superiors (cc. 708–709)

Regular assemblies of major superiors date back to the late nineteenth and early twentieth centuries. They originated in Germany and France. At that time, they had no foundation in canon law. The 1917 Code of Canon Law does not contain any norms on conferences of major superiors. At the International Congress of States of Perfection in 1950, Pope Pius XII recommended that major superiors hold regular assemblies to promote cooperation and mutual assistance, which resulted in a large number of conferences of major superiors being founded, including in the United States and Canada. The Second Vatican Council states in *Perfectae Caritatis* 23 that conferences or councils of major superiors should be encouraged. *Ecclesiae Sanctae* 43 and *Mutuae Relationes* 61–65 emphasize the importance of assemblies of major superiors for collaboration with bishops' conferences.

The 1983 Code of Canon Law leaves it up to major superiors to form conferences and councils (see c. 708), while maintaining the autonomy of the individual institutes. Conferences and councils of major superiors cannot make decisions that are binding for individual institutes. The Code states as purposes of conferences and councils of major superiors (see c. 708):

- to achieve more fully the purpose of the individual institutes
- to transact common affairs
- to establish appropriate coordination and cooperation with the bishops' conferences and with individual bishops

Conferences of major superiors are erected as a juridic person by the Apostolic See, which needs to approve their statutes and under the supreme direction of which they remain (see c. 709). In the United States, there are three conferences of major superiors: The Conference of Major Superiors of Men (CMSM) was established in 1957. The Conference of Major Superiors of Women (CMSW) was established in 1959 and changed its name in 1971 to Leadership Conference of Women Religious (LCWR). Furthermore, the Council of Major Superiors of Women Religious (CMSWR) was established in 1992. In Canada, there is one conference of major superiors for men and women religious: The Canadian Religious Conference (CRC) was established in 1954.

Chapter Three

Secular Institutes (cc. 710–730)

Secular institutes are a recent form of consecrated life that emerged in the twentieth century. Members of a secular institute commit themselves to the evangelical counsels as religious do, but they do not live in communities. Usually, at least, as some secular institutes do have some kind of community life but without the enclosure of a religious institute. Members of a secular institute live in the world and pursue their own occupations. They do not wear a habit or a garb, so they are not immediately recognizable to the outside world as members of a secular institute.

Although secular institutes did not emerge until the twentieth century, the first attempt to establish a form of life similar to today's secular institutes was made in northern Italy in the sixteenth century. Together with a group of fellow women, Angela Merici (1474–1540) founded the Company of Saint Ursula, which received papal recognition in 1535. The members of this company were unmarried women who remained in their family homes. They wished to live a committed Christian life in the world and to engage in charitable work by establishing a school for girls from families in need. They did not take public vows, which would have required them to live in a cloistered community. It was recommended that they take private vows. However, the time was not yet ripe for such an innovation. The external demands of such a way of life and the loss of a leading personality after the death of Angela Merici led the Company of Saint Ursula to move in a different direction as early as the seventeenth century. In 1618, the community was transformed into an order with solemn vows and strict enclosure, giving rise to the Order of Saint Ursula (Ursulines). In 1958, the Secular Institute of Saint Angela Merici was founded in northern Italy, intentionally following the spirit of the foundation of Angela Merici.

The 1917 Code of Canon Law did not recognize secular institutes. Secular institutes were recognized in canon law for the first time with the apostolic constitution *Provida Mater Ecclesia* of Pope Pius XII of February 2, 1947.[1] The members of secular institutes lead a consecrated life with full commitment to the evangelical counsels, which distinguishes them from associations of the faithful, but under the conditions of the world, which distinguishes them from religious institutes. Further details followed in the motu proprio *Primo Feliciter* of the same pope of March 12, 1948,[2] to which the Congregation for Religious gave implementing regulations in the instruction *Cum Sanctissimis* of March 19, 1948. These documents emphasize an apostolic life in the world and with the means of the world as essential characteristics of secular institutes. The Second Vatican Council addresses secular institutes in *Perfectae Caritatis* 11. The 1983 Code of Canon Law includes secular institutes, along with religious institutes, among the institutes of consecrated life and defines them as institutes "in which the Christian faithful, living in the world, strive for the perfection of charity and seek to contribute to the sanctification of the world, especially from within" (c. 710). Membership in a secular institute "does not change the member's proper canonical condition among the people of God, whether lay or clerical" (c. 711). A member of a secular institute is not a religious. They remain a lay person or a secular priest. The

[1] *AAS* 39 (1947): 114–24.

[2] *AAS* 40 (1948): 283–86.

term "consecrated secular" is sometimes used to refer to a member of a secular institute.

Further reading: Fermina Álvarez Alonso, "Consecration and Secular Life in the Second Vatican Council: The Contribution of the Secular Institutes," *Jur* 76 (2016): 43–67; Jean Beyer, *A New Way of Apostolic Consecrated Life: The Secular Institute* (Pontificia Università Gregoriana, 1967); Julián Herranz Casado, "The Evolution of Secular Institutes," *Jur* 25 (1965): 129–62; Andrea Michl, "'In saeculo et ex saeculo': Characteristics of the Secular Institutes," *Warszawskie Studia Teologiczne* 34 (2021): 196–211; B. M. Ottinger and A. S. Fischer, eds., *Secular Institutes in the 1983 Code: A New Vocation in the Church* (Christian Classics, 1988).

1. Sacred Bonds (c. 712)

The constitutions of a secular institute determine the nature of the bonds by which the members assume the evangelical counsels:

- *vow*: "a deliberate and free promise made to God about a possible and better good [that] must be fulfilled by reason of the virtue of religion" (c. 1191 §1)
- *promise*: "a single act of self-giving to Christ, which expresses and characterizes the choice of evangelical radicality in the secular state [and which] also involves a commitment to remain faithful to the words given and to fulfill the substance of the promise, by virtue of justice"[3]
- *oath*: "the invocation of the divine name in witness to the truth" (c. 1199 §1)

[3] Melanie S. Reyes, "A Comparative Study of Sacred Bonds in Institutes of Consecrated Life," *Philippiniana Sacra* 54 (2019): 223.

Furthermore, constitutions are to determine the content of the obligations assumed by the bonds on the basis of cc. 599–601. The commitment to the evangelical counsel of chastity entails, as in religious institutes, "the obligation of perfect continence in celibacy" (c. 599). What is assumed by the commitment to the evangelical counsels of poverty (see c. 718) and obedience (see c. 717) differs significantly between religious and secular institutes, since their proper secularity must always be preserved.

Further reading: Melanie S. Reyes, "A Comparative Study of Sacred Bonds in Institutes of Consecrated Life," *Philippiniana Sacra* 54 (2019): 219–40.

2. Apostolic Activity (c. 713)

The apostolate of members of secular institutes, like that of religious, consists above all in the witness of their consecrated life. They are called to "strive to imbue all things with the spirit of the gospel for the strengthening and growth of the Body of Christ" (c. 713 §1). Lay members are called to give "witness of a Christian life and of fidelity toward their own consecration" (c. 713 §2). They should also offer their cooperation in the service of the Christian community. The clerical members give witness of their consecrated life in the presbyterate and in their pastoral activity (see c. 713 §3). They are normally incardinated in the diocese to which they belong, unless the institute itself has the right of incardination by virtue of grant of the Apostolic See (see c. 266 §3). The clerics of a secular institute incardinated in a diocese are subject to the bishop, except in matters concerning their consecrated life (see c. 715 §1). If, on the other hand, they are incardinated in the institute, they are dependent on the bishop in the manner of religious (see c. 715 §2).

3. Governance (c. 717)

In the case of secular institutes, the Code of Canon Law does not speak of superiors, as in the case of religious institutes, but of moderators. It is left to the constitutions to determine the manner of governance, as well as the manner of designation (appointment or election) of moderators and their term of office (see c. 717 §1), both for the institute as a whole and for its parts, if there are any. There is only one specific requirement in universal law, namely, that the supreme moderator of a secular institute must be definitively incorporated into it (see c. 717 §2). The supreme moderator is to be held responsible for the unity of spirit in the institute and for the promotion of the active participation of the members (see c. 717 §3).

The constitutions are to describe the authority the moderators have over the members. In secular institutes, the vow of obedience is less extensive than in religious institutes. Usually, the moderators are consulted only in the case of major life decisions, such as career changes or relocation.

4. Administration of Temporal Goods (c. 718)

Secular institutes are public juridic persons. Their temporal goods are therefore ecclesiastical goods (see c. 1257 §1), and the norms of the fifth book of the Code of Canon Law on ecclesiastical goods apply. To establish further norms concerning temporal goods, which must express and foster evangelical poverty, is a matter for proper law (see c. 718).

The regulations concerning the goods of members may vary from institute to institute. In secular institutes there is no full renunciation of property or cession of the administration of the members' goods. Usually, members of secular institutes earn their own living and are responsible for their own social security and pension. They contribute financially to the interests of the institute. The amount of this contribution and what is financed by it varies according to whether the members live in community or not. There are secular institutes where members work for the institute. Like religious, they place themselves and their work at the service of the institute. In this case, the institute is responsible for the maintenance and social security of the members. The financial obligations of the institute towards the members who work for it are to be determined by proper law (see c. 718).

5. Spiritual Life (c. 719)

Each secular institute has its own spiritual identity, and each member has his own personal spirituality. However, c. 719 enumerates some basics of the spiritual life which are recommended to members so that their union with Christ nourishes their apostolic activity:

- prayer
- Bible reading
- annual spiritual retreat
- daily participation in the Eucharistic celebration, if possible
- frequent reception of the sacrament of penance
- necessary direction of conscience
- other spiritual exercises according to proper law

A comparison with the norm on the spiritual life of religious (see c. 663) reveals similarities but also differences. For lay members of a secular institute, there is no obligation under universal law to carry out the Liturgy of the Hours, although such an obligation may be included in the proper law. Clerical members are obliged to carry out the Liturgy of the Hours according to c. 276 §2,3°. It is not clear why veneration of the Mother of God, contemplation of divine things, adoration, and frequent reception of the Body of Christ is recommended only to religious and not to members of secular institutes, especially since these are common forms of piety that are not practiced only by religious.

Regarding reception of the sacrament of penance as well as necessary direction of conscience, members of secular institutes must be allowed the due freedom (see c. 719 §§3–4). They may seek direction of conscience from the moderators, but only if they wish.

6. Admission and Formation (cc. 720–725)

The admission of new members is a successive incorporation, divided into a period of probation, temporary incorporation, and perpetual or definitive incorporation. The right to admit candidates to the period of probation, as well as to temporary, perpetual, or definitive incorporation, belongs to the major moderator with their council, according to the norm of the constitutions (see c. 720).

One who wants to be admitted to the period of probation must have the maturity necessary to lead rightly the proper life of the institute (see c. 721 §3). Secular institutes usually do not have a community life. Candidates live much more independently than religious, which requires a certain degree of maturity. The basic requirements for admission into an institute of consecrated life are (see c. 597 §1):

- being a Catholic
- right intention
- qualities required by universal law and proper law
- no impediments

Impediments to valid admission are listed in c. 721 §1. A candidate cannot be validly admitted who:

- has not yet attained the age of majority,
- is bound by a sacred bond in an institute of consecrated life or who is incorporated in a society of apostolic life, or
- is a spouse, while the marriage continues to exist.

In secular institutes, the age of majority is required for admission to initial probation. This means that the minimum age is higher than for admission to the novitiate of religious institutes. This reflects common practice, since the admission of underage persons to a religious institute is most likely an exception. Those who are bound by a sacred bond in an institute of consecrated life or who are incorporated in a society of apostolic life cannot be admitted. In this case, a transfer according to c. 730 is to be carried out. Since members of a secular institute assume the evangelical counsel of chastity, no spouse can be admitted as long as a valid marriage exists. Constitutions may impose other impediments, also for validity, or conditions. They may also set a higher minimum age and a maximum age. Constitutions must also define the manner and length of the period of probation, which must not be less than two years (see c. 722 §3). The period of probation must be organized so that the candidates understand their own vocation and the vocation proper to the institute. They are to be trained in the spirit and way of life of the institute (see c. 722 §1), and they are to be guided to lead a life according to the evangelical counsels and to transform their whole life into the apostolate proper to the institute (see c. 722 §2).

At the end of the period of probation, a candidate must either be admitted to incorporation at their request, in accordance with the provisions of the constitutions, or they must leave the institute (see c. 723 §1). The first admission is always temporary. It must last at least five years and may be renewed in accordance with the provisions of the constitutions (see c. 723 §2). Universal law does not provide for a maximum period, but constitutions may provide for one. At the end of the period of temporary incorporation, the candidate can be admitted to perpetual or definitive incorporation (see c. 723 §3). Definitive incorporation means that the candidate wishes to make a lifelong commitment to the evangelical counsels, but rather than making a perpetual commitment, they renew the temporary commitment on an ongoing basis. The legal effects of definitive incorporation are the same as those of perpetual incorporation according to the provisions of the constitutions (see c. 723 §4).

The period of probation is the initial formation in the institute. After assuming temporary bonds, formation should continue (see c. 724 §1). The details are to be regulated in the constitutions. The ongoing spiritual formation of the members should be a concern of the moderators (see c. 724 §2).

An institute may associate, by means of bonds to be defined in its constitutions, other faithful, including married persons, who live in the spirit of the institute and participate in its mission (see c. 725).[4]

7. Separation from the Institute (cc. 726–730)

A member is free to leave the institute at the end of the period of temporary incorporation. They may be excluded from the renewal of the bonds for a just cause by the major moderator after consultation with their council (see c. 726 §1). During temporary incorporation, a member may, at their request, receive from the supreme moderator, with the consent of their council, an indult of departure for a just cause (see

[4] For further details, see María V. Hernández Rodríguez, "I fedeli associati agli istituti secolari: Genesi e fonti del can. 725," *ME* 126 (2001): 437–57.

c. 726 §2). A member who, after perpetual incorporation, wishes to leave the institute for a very grave reason and after serious reflection before God, may request an indult of departure through the supreme moderator, in the case of institutes of pontifical right, from the Apostolic See, or in the case of institutes of diocesan right, either from the competent diocesan bishop or from the Apostolic See, according to the provisions of the constitution (see c. 727 §1). If the member wishing to leave is a cleric and if they are incardinated in the institute, an indult of departure will not be granted until they have found a bishop who will incardinate them in his diocese, or at least accept them experimentally, or until they at the same time request laicization (see cc. 693; 727 §2). Once the indult of departure has been lawfully granted, the bonds, as well as the rights and obligations deriving from them, cease (see c. 728). According to the wording of c. 728, there is no right to reject an indult of departure when it is announced.

With regard to dismissal from a secular institute, c. 729 refers to the provisions applicable to religious institutes in cc. 694 §1,1-2°, 695, and 697–701. A dismissal ipso facto occurs in the case of notorious defection from the Catholic faith (see c. 694 §1,1°) and in the case of marriage or attempted marriage, even if only civil (c. 694 §1,2°). Since secular institutes do not have the obligation of common life, there can be no unlawful absence from a religious house in a secular institute, and c. 694 §1,3° does not apply to members of a secular institute. A member of a secular institute must be dismissed in the cases provided for in c. 695. The constitutions may provide for other causes of dismissal, which must be sufficiently serious, external, imputable, and juridically proven. The procedure set forth in cc. 699–700 must be followed. With regard to the legal effects of the dismissal, c. 701 is applicable.

Regarding the transfer of a member from one secular institute to another (see c. 730), cc. 684 §§1–2.4 and 685 regarding the transfer of a religious are applicable. Omitted is c. 684

§3, as there are no autonomous monasteries in secular institutes. Regarding a transfer to or from a religious institute or a society of apostolic life, the matter must be submitted to the Apostolic See, whose mandates must be observed (see c. 730).

Part II

Societies of Apostolic Life

Chapter Four

Societies of Apostolic Life
(cc. 731–746)

Members of a society of apostolic life lead a common life to pursue their proper common apostolic purpose and to strive for perfection of charity according to the constitutions without religious vows (see c. 731 §1). In some societies, members commit themselves to the evangelical counsels through private vows, a promise, an oath, or a contract as defined in the constitutions (see c. 731 §2).

The oldest society without vows is the Oratory of St. Philip Neri, founded in 1575. Philip Neri (d. 1595) worked as a priest in Rome. He met regularly with other priests for prayer, spiritual reading, and spiritual discourse. At first the meetings were held in his home and later in oratories provided by various monasteries. Hence the name of the society. The members devoted themselves to pastoral and charitable work. They adopted the community life of religious orders but did not take public vows. The first women's society without vows were the Daughters of Charity of St. Vincent de Paul, founded by Vincent de Paul (d. 1660) and Louise de Marillac (d. 1660). In the small town of Châtillon-sur-Chalaronne in France, they founded a community of women dedicated to helping the poor and sick. The members lived a common life without taking public vows. They received papal approval in 1654.

The 1917 Code of Canon Law spoke of societies of common life without vows (*societates in communi viventium sine votis*) and did not include their members among religious in the proper sense (see c. 673 §1 CIC/1917). The 1983 Code of Canon Law lists societies of apostolic life in a common section with institutes of consecrated life. The members of a society of apostolic life do not commit themselves through a public bond to the evangelical counsels. This distinguishes them from members of institutes of consecrated life. Nevertheless, there are structural similarities, so that c. 732 refers to cc. 578–597 and 606 concerning institutes of consecrated life, which are applied to societies of apostolic life, without prejudice to the particular nature of each society. The references in c. 732 cover the following areas of law:

- c. 578: patrimony
- cc. 579–585: erection, aggregation, mergers and unions, confederations and federations, changes, suppression, and erection and suppression of parts
- c. 586: just autonomy
- c. 587: constitutions and other proper law
- cc. 588–595: typology
- c. 596: superiors and chapters
- c. 597: basic requirements for admission
- c. 606: equal applicability of the law

In addition, the following norms from the law of institutes of consecrated life apply to societies in which members assume the evangelical counsels through some bond:

- cc. 598–601: evangelical counsels
- c. 602: communion of life

In various individual norms, further canons are borrowed from the law for religious institutes for societies of apostolic life.

Further reading: Thomas J. Finn, "An Old Entity—A New Name: Societies of Apostolic Life," *StudCan* 20 (1986): 439–56.

1. Houses and Local Communities (c. 733)

Societies of apostolic life can have houses and local communities, although neither term is defined in universal law. Proper law may contain more detailed provisions. In principle, a house has a permanent character, while a local community is more likely to be a temporary common residence during a particular apostolate.

The erection of a house and the establishment of a local community are carried out by the competent authority of the society according to the constitutions. The prior written consent of the diocesan bishop is required (see c. 733 §1). Consent to the erection of a house includes the right to have an oratory, where the Eucharist is celebrated[1] and reserved (see c. 733 §2). A lawfully erected house is, by virtue of the law itself, a public juridic person in canon law (see c. 116 §2). This does not apply to the establishment of a local community, but the competent ecclesiastical authority may confer this status on it if the conditions are met.

The diocesan bishop must be consulted before a house or local community is suppressed (see c. 733 §1).

2. Governance (cc. 734, 738)

The governance of a society of apostolic life is to be determined in its constitutions (see c. 734). Without prejudice to the specific nature of a society, cc. 617–633 on superiors and their councils and on chapters of religious institutes apply, though universal law does not speak of superiors but of moderators.

[1] At least twice a month, as far as possible, according to c. 934 §2.

With regard to internal governance, all members are subject to their proper moderators in accordance with the provisions of the constitutions (see c. 738 §1). Regarding public worship, pastoral care, and other apostolic works, members are also subject to the diocesan bishop (see c. 738 §2). In this regard, canons 679–683 from the law for religious institutes are to be observed.

Further reading: Showri Raju Yetukuri, "General Governance in the Societies of Apostolic Life," *Scientia Canonica* 3 (2020): 99–141.

3. Admission and Formation (cc. 735–736)

Admission, probation, incorporation, and formation of members is to be determined in the proper law (see c. 735 §1). Regarding admission, cc. 642–645 from the law for religious institutes apply (see c. 735 §2). The manner of probation and formation is to be determined by proper law. Formation shall be doctrinal, spiritual, and apostolic according to the purpose and character of a society. It shall help the members to recognize their own vocation, and it shall suitably prepare them for the mission and life of the society (see c. 735 §3).

Clerical members of clerical societies of apostolic life are incardinated in the society, unless the constitutions provide otherwise (see c. 736 §1). If a clerical member is not incardinated in the society, his relations with his bishop are to be regulated in the constitutions or in special agreements (see c. 738 §3). Regarding the program of studies and the reception of ordination, the provisions for secular clerics are to be observed,[2] without prejudice to the provisions of the society's own regulations (see c. 736 §2).

[2] For English-speaking Canada: Canadian Conference of Catholic Bishops, *Program for Priestly Formation (Ratio formationis sacerdotalis nationalis) for English-speaking Canada* (CCCB, 2022). For the United States: United States

4. Obligations and Rights (cc. 737, 739–740)

The obligations and rights of members are to be determined in the constitutions (see c. 737). In addition, members are bound by the common obligations of clerics, unless the nature of the matter or the context requires otherwise (see c. 739), and they are obliged to lead a common life according to the norms of the proper law in their own house or local community. It is for the proper law to establish norms concerning lawful absence (see c. 740). The society has the duty to guide the members to the end of their proper vocation according to the constitutions (see c. 737).

5. Administration of Temporal Goods (c. 741)

Societies, their parts, and their houses (not their local communities) are public juridic persons (see c. 116 §1), and therefore their temporal goods are ecclesiastical goods (see c. 1257 §1), so that they are bound by the norms of cc. 1258–1310. They are able to acquire, retain, administer, and alienate temporal goods (see c. 1254 §1). Regarding their administration, norms are to be established in proper law. In addition, the followings canons from the law for religious institutes apply (see c. 714 §1):

- c. 636: finance officer
- c. 638: ordinary and extraordinary administration, and alienation
- c. 639: liability for debts and obligations

Members retain their capability to acquire, possess, administer, and dispose temporal goods according to the norms of proper law (see c. 741 §2), as they do not take a vow of poverty.

Conference of Catholic Bishops, *Program of Priestly Formation in the United States of America*, 6th ed. (USCCB, 2022).

What they acquire on behalf of the society is acquired by the society according to the norms of proper law.

6. Separation from the Society (cc. 742–746)

Norms concerning departure and dismissal of a member who has not yet been definitively incorporated are to be laid down in the constitutions (see c. 742).

An indult of departure for a definitively incorporated member can be obtained from the supreme moderator with the consent of the council, unless this faculty is reserved to the Apostolic See according to the constitutions (see c. 743). As members of a society of apostolic life usually do not take vows, no intervention from the Apostolic See is required. In societies where members do take vows, the constitutions usually refer cases of departure of definitively incorporated members to the Apostolic See. If the member requesting an indult of departure is a cleric, the indult may be granted only if they have found a bishop willing to incardinate them in his diocese, or at least to receive them experimentally, or if they also request laicization along with the indult of departure (see c. 693). With an indult of departure lawfully obtained, the rights and obligations deriving from incorporation cease.

Permission for a definitively incorporated member to transfer to another society of apostolic life can be granted by the supreme moderator with the consent of their council (see c. 744 §1). The manner and duration of the time of probation in the new society is to be determined by its proper law. Before definitive incorporation in the new society, the member retains the right to return. If it concerns a transfer to or from an institute of consecrated life, the matter must be submitted to the Apostolic See, whose mandates must be observed (see c. 744 §2).

A definitively incorporated member can obtain an indult to live outside the society for up to three years from the supreme moderator with the consent of their council (see c. 745). With such an indult lawfully obtained, the rights and obligations that cannot be reconciled with the new condition of the member are suspended. The member remains under the care of their proper moderators. If the member is a cleric, consent of the ordinary of the place where they will reside is required.

Regarding the dismissal of a definitively incorporated member, cc. 694–704 from the law for religious institutes are to be applied (see c. 746). Appropriate adaptations must be made where necessary. This is especially the case where these canons refer to sacred bonds, for example, in c. 696 §1, where causes for dismissal are named.

Appendix

Recourse in Administrative Matters

Canon law provides for the possibility of recourse in administrative matters. Members of institutes of consecrated life and societies of apostolic life can appeal against decrees of their superiors by which they consider themselves aggrieved. The same applies to juridic persons: houses, provinces, institutes, and societies have the right to appeal against decrees issued by a bishop or a dicastery of the Apostolic See.

Administrative Recourse (cc. 1732–1739)

The norms on administrative recourse are applicable to "all singular administrative acts which are given in the external forum outside a trial excepting those which have been issued by the Roman Pontiff or an ecumenical council" (c. 1732). Therefore, not object of an administrative recourse are:

- general decrees and instructions, as they are not singular acts;
- ecclesiastical laws as well as constitutions and other proper law of an institute of consecrated life and society of apostolic life, as they are not administrative acts;[1]

[1] Laws or general decrees issued by legislators below the level of the pope can be challenged before the Dicastery for Legislative Texts. At the request

- judicial sentences and decrees of a tribunal besides a sentence (e.g., decree of removal of a procurator or an advocate) as they are not administrative acts;[2]
- preparatory acts for a decree (e.g., canonical warnings as preparatory acts for a decree of dismissal);
- administrative acts regarding the internal forum (e.g., issued by the Apostolic Penitentiary);
- acts of administration that do not constitute an act of executive power (e.g., contracts in the context of the administration of temporal goods);[3]
- decrees of the pope or an ecumenical council, as the pope and with him the college of bishops hold the supreme power in the church, as no recourse against their decisions is possible.[4]

There is no legal definition of the term "singular administrative act" in the Code. The Code deals with singular administrative acts in cc. 35–93. A singular administrative act can be a decree including a precept (see cc. 48–58) or a rescript (see cc. 59–75) issued by a person who possesses executive power within the limits of their competence. A decree is "an administrative act issued by a competent executive authority in which a decision is given or a provision is made for a particular case according to the norms of law. Of their nature,

---

of an interested party, the dicastery determines whether they are in conformity with the universal law of the church (see PE 181).

[2] Such a decree can be challenged in accordance with the procedural norms for tribunals proceedings.

[3] Controversies arising from acts of administration fall into the competence of ordinary ecclesiastical tribunals.

[4] While decrees of an ecumenical council are not relevant in praxis, decrees confirmed by the pope do occur in praxis to settle a matter quickly and definitively without the possibility of a recourse. Although such a procedure is efficient, it deprives the person concerned of any possibility of legal protection.

these decisions or provisions do not presuppose a petition made by someone" (c. 48). A precept is a special form of a decree "which directly and legitimately enjoins a specific person or persons to do or omit something, especially in order to urge the observance of law" (c. 49). A decree must be issued in writing and, for its validity, give the reasons at least summarily expressed if it is a decision (see c. 51). A rescript "grants a privilege, dispensation, or other favor at someone's request" (c. 59 §1). It is to be issued in writing by the competent executive authority. Singular administrative acts that can be challenged through administrative recourse are not limited to decrees and rescripts. Therefore, decisions by lay religious superiors, who are not ordinaries and therefore do not possess executive power, can be challenged through administrative recourse, as their decisions are to be considered acts of administrative power (see c. 596 §§1 and 3).[5] The norms on administrative recourse use the term "decree" to refer to singular administrative acts in the sense of c. 1732.

An administrative recourse is furthermore possible if an executive authority fails to act. Whenever universal law or proper law of an institute orders a decree to be issued or an interested party legitimately proposes a petition or recourse to obtain a decree, the competent authority is to provide for the matter within three months from the receipt of the petition or recourse unless another time period is prescribed (see c. 57 §1). When this time period has passed and a decree has not been given, the response is presumed to be negative, and an administrative recourse can be presented (see c. 57 §2).

Before an administrative recourse is lodged, it is desirable that the parties involved should try mediation. The norms on alternative dispute resolution in c. 1733 reflect basic principles of conflict resolution strategies in the New Testament (see

[5] See Apostolic Signatura, *Litterae* of February 9, 1988, Prot. N. 19764/88 VT, in Thomas J. Paprocki, "Section I: Recourse Against administrative Decrees [cc. 1732–1739]," in Beal et al., *New Commentary*, 1823.

Matt 18:15–17). "Whenever a person considers himself aggrieved by a decree, it is particularly desirable that the person and the author of the decree avoid any contention and take care to seek an equitable solution by common counsel, possibly using the mediation and effort of wise persons to avoid or settle the controversy in a suitable way" (c. 1733). The requirements for an administrative recourse are low: it is sufficient that a person feels aggrieved by a decree. If this is the case, litigation should be avoided as far as possible. Instead, an equitable solution between the parties should be found. Both parties can come to this equitable solution between themselves, but mediators can also be called in. The attempt to reach an equitable solution is not obligatory. There are cases in which an attempt at mediation makes sense; in other cases it may seem futile from the start. It should also be noted that the time limits for lodging an administrative recourse begin to run even if an attempt at mediation has been made.

Mediation can take an institutional form (see c. 1733 §2) as a bishops' conference can determine that each diocese should establish in a stable manner an office or council to seek and suggest equitable solutions. If a bishops' conference has not established such an office or council, it is up to the discretion of each individual diocesan bishop to do so in his own territory.[6] Supreme moderators can do the same for their institutes of consecrated life or societies of apostolic life.[7] Mediators can be individual persons or a group of persons. It is up to the bishops' conferences or individual diocesan bishops to determine the details of the mediation process. In any case, mediators can only make suggestions for dispute resolution, which the parties involved can accept or reject. They are not arbitrators and therefore are not authorized to rule or decide on the merits. Mediation can still be sought even after the formal process of administrative recourse has been initiated.

[6] The USCCB has left the decision to the individual diocesan bishops.

[7] See Miller and Jaramillo, *Procedural Handbook*, 223–27.

Both procedures can be performed in parallel. The hierarchical superior who has to decide on an administrative recourse should encourage the parties involved to seek alternative dispute resolution if they see a prospect of success (see c. 1733 §3). Even if there is no prospect of success, an alternative dispute resolution can be useful, at least from a pastoral point of view. The person concerned thereby has an official ecclesiastical institution that listens to them and takes their concerns seriously.

Another expression of amicable conflict resolution is the obligation to seek a revocation or modification from the author of the decree in question before any recourse to the hierarchical superior (see c. 1734 §1). The petition must be submitted in writing within a peremptory period of ten useful days from the legitimate notification of the decree (see c. 1734 §§1–2). Peremptory period means that after its expiry, the right to lodge an administrative recourse extinguishes. Useful time (*tempus utile*) means that the time period of ten days does not run for a person who is unaware or unable to act (see c. 201 §2). The time period of ten days begins after the legitimate notification of the decree, that is, when the recipient becomes aware of the decree. If the recipient is unaware of the decree, the time period does not run. The burden of proof of notification lies with the author of the decree, as it is impossible for the recipient to prove that he did not receive the decree. A decree is deemed to have been lawfully promulgated if it has actually reached the recipient or if it has reached them in such a way that they could have become aware of the decree, for example, by placing it in a letter box or by notifying them that a letter is ready for collection at the post office. Therefore, refusal of acceptance will not be a bar to notification. It is also possible to hand over the written decree personally or to read the text of the decree to the person to whom it is addressed in the presence of a notary or two witnesses (see c. 55). To ensure that the recipient of the decree cannot claim that they were unaware of the time limit for recourse, it is advisable to provide the decree with instructions on the right to recourse. The recipient of the decree may be considered unable to act for subjective or objective reasons. They can be unable to act because of illness, for instance, or because of absence of their advocate. If the last day of the ten-day period is a Sunday, the end of the period is postponed to the next working day. When the petition to revoke or to modify a decree is proposed, suspension of the execution of the decree is also understood to be requested (see c. 1734 §1).

A petition to revoke or to modify a decree is not required in the following cases:

- *recourse proposed to a bishop against decrees issued by authorities subject to him (see c. 1734 §3, 1°):* This applies, for example, to decrees issued by officials of the diocesan curia. In this case, a petition to revoke or to modify a decree is not required, and an administrative recourse can be presented directly to the bishop. According to the jurisprudence of the Apostolic Signatura, this does not apply to decrees issued by vicars general or episcopal vicars (e.g., episcopal vicar for religious).[8] In these cases, a petition to revoke or to modify a decree must be presented before an administrative recourse can be filed, either to the vicar general or episcopal vicar, or to the diocesan bishop.[9]

[8] See Apostolic Signatura, *Sententia definitiva* c. Stankiewicz of October 22, 2014, Prot. N. 48116/13 CA, in *Ius Communionis* 5 (2017): 309–24: "*In ordine ad impugnationem decreti Vicarii generalis vel Vicarii episcopalis observari debet praescriptum can. 1734, §§ 1–2, scilicet de remonstratione sive coram Vicario generali vel Vicario episcopali, sive coram ipso Episcopo facienda ante recursum hierarchicum, non autem can. 1734, § 3, n. 1, id est de remonstratione tunc omittenda*" (321).

[9] See Apostolic Signatura, *Decretum Secretarii* of September 4, 2015, Prot. N. 50325/15 CA, in *Jur* 77 (2021): 465–70: "*Iurisprudentia H.S.T. admittit huiusmodi in casu remonstrationem sive apud eundem Vicarium generalem sive apud Exc.mum Episcopum*" (467).

- *recourse against a decree that decides an administrative recourse unless the bishop gave the decision (see c. 1734 §3, 2°):* In the case of a decision on an administrative recourse, the author of the decision is already aware of the dispute and the arguments of the parties, so that reconsideration of the decision by the same authority would not be beneficial but would only delay the process. It is not immediately clear why the decision of a bishop on a recourse against a decision of a subordinate administrative authority is an exception. It is possible that the purpose of this exception is to ensure that a case will be decided at a local level whenever possible and that an appeal to the Apostolic See will be made only when there is no prospect of resolution of the case locally.
- *recourse proposed according to c. 57 or c. 1735 (see c. 1734 §3, 3°):* In these two cases, a petition to revoke or modify a decision would be futile. Canon 57 deals with cases in which an executive authority fails to act, and a negative response is presumed. As there is no decree, there can be no petition to revoke or modify it. Canon 1735 deals with the decision on a petition to revoke or modify a decree. An administrative recourse against this decision can be made to the hierarchical superior. Otherwise, an infinite loop would occur at this point.
- *recourse against a decree of dismissal of a member of a religious institute (see c. 700), of a secular institute (see c. 729), or of a society of apostolic life (see c. 746):* Before a decree of dismissal can be issued, a dismissal procedure must be conducted in which the member has an adequate opportunity to defend himself (see cc. 698–700). Therefore, it is very unlikely that the superior who issued the decree of dismissal will change their mind and revoke the decree after a petition from the member.

If the petition to revoke or to modify a decree is obligatory but has not been presented, the hierarchical superior of the author of the decree can reject an administrative recourse for this reason. However, they are also free to accept an unlawfully lodged administrative recourse ex officio and to rule on it in accordance with c. 1739.[10]

The author of the decree has thirty days from receipt of the petition to revoke or to modify a decree to decide on this petition (see c. 1735). This period is considerably shorter than the three months generally provided for in c. 57 §1. The shorter period is intended to speed up the procedure. The author of the decree is already familiar with the case as such, and they only need to consider the new grounds put forward. The author of the decree in question must issue a new decree either revoking or modifying the old decree or deciding that the petition must be rejected. The time limits for making recourse (see c. 1737 §2) run from the notification of the new decree. If the competent authority does not issue a new decree within the thirty-day period, the time limit for recourse begins on the thirtieth day.

A petition to revoke or to modify a decree does not automatically lead to the suspension of the execution of the decree in question, unless the suspension of execution of a decree is prescribed by law in the case of an administrative recourse (see c. 1736 §1). The latter applies in the case of an administrative recourse against a decree of dismissal of a member of a religious institute (see c. 700), secular institute (see c. 729), or

[10] See Apostolic Signatura, *Decretum definitivum* of June 24, 2014, Prot. N. 47546/13 CA, in *PRC* 112 (2023): 110–23: "*Exc.mus Recurrens contendit Superiorissam Generalem revocationem vel emendationem decreti omisisse petendam. . . . Quidquid est, recte adnotat Rev.dus Promotor Iustitiae Substitutus quod iuxta communem H.S.T. iurisprudentiam Congregatio pro Institutis vitae consecratae et Societatibus vitae apostolicae, uti Superior hierarchicus Exc.mi Episcopi quoad instituta religiosa, etiam recursum haud legitime exhibitum ex officio accipere, pertractare ac definire potest, praescripto can. 1739 utens*" (116).

society of apostolic life (see c. 746); against a decree that imposes or declares a penalty (see c. 1353); against a decree of removal of a pastor (see c. 1747 §3); and against a decree of transfer of a pastor (see c. 1752).[11] The author of the decree in question must decide on the suspension of the execution of the decree within ten days of receipt of the petition in cases where the petition does not have an automatic suspensive effect (see c. 1736 §1), as pursuant to c. 1734 §1, suspension of execution is deemed to have been requested in any case. If they refuse to suspend the execution or do not act within the ten-day period, the suspension may be granted by their hierarchical superior, but "only for grave reasons and always cautiously so that the salvation of souls suffers no harm" (c. 1736 §2). If after the petition to revoke or to modify a decree an administrative recourse is proposed, the hierarchical superior must decide whether the suspension is to be confirmed or revoked (see c. 1736 §3). If no recourse is proposed within the time limits, the suspension of the execution ceases (see c. 1736 §4).

Administrative recourse can be made by a (physical or a juridic) person who claims to have been aggrieved by a decree for any just reason (see c. 1737 §1). Standing to make an administrative recourse is held by anyone who claims that a right or an interest has been violated that is personal, direct, current, and at least indirectly protected by law.[12] A just reason is sufficient. This may be an allegation of a violation of the law in the proceedings or in the decision on the merits, or simply an

[11] In the latter two cases, if the pastor is a religious, different procedures apply (see c. 682 §2) and the exceptions are not applicable.

[12] See Apostolic Signatura, *Decretum definitivum* of November 21, 1987, Prot. N. 17447/85 CA, in *Comm* 20 (1988) 88–94: "*Locutione 'gravatum esse contendit' haud obscure indicatur fundamentum iuridicum legitimationis activae. Gravamen in casu praesupponit recurrentem ius aliquod subiectivum aut saltem interesse habere; quod quidem interesse, ut fundamentum praebeat actioni, intelligi nequit quodcumque, sed debet esse, ut doctrina docet, personale, directum, actuale et a lege, saltem indirecte, tutelatum.*"

allegation that the decision is not opportune. Recourse is to be made to the hierarchical superior of the person who issued the decree in question (see c. 1737 §1).[13] The recourse may be addressed directly to the hierarchical superior[14] or to the person who issued the decree in question and who must transmit it immediately to their hierarchical superior.

Recourse must be made within the peremptory time limit of fifteen useful days (see c. 1737 §2). In cases where a petition to revoke or to modify is not required, the time limit starts to run from the date of notification of the decree. If such a petition is required, the time limit starts to run from the date of notification of the decree by which the petition was decided or from the thirtieth day after the petition was proposed if there is no answer. If the time limit has elapsed, the hierarchical superior can reject an administrative recourse for this reason. However, they are also free to accept an administrative recourse that was filed late and to rule on it in accordance with c. 1739. If the suspension of execution of a decree is not prescribed by law and has not already been granted after a petition to revoke or to modify the decree, the hierarchical superior can grant suspension for a grave cause, "yet cautiously so that the salvation of souls suffers no harm" (c. 1737 §3).

One who makes an administrative recourse has the right to use an advocate or procurator, who can also be appointed ex officio if the hierarchical superior thinks it is necessary (see c. 1738). Nothing is said about the qualifications and duties

[13] The hierarchical superior of a diocesan bishop is the pope. Therefore, a recourse against a decree of the bishop goes to the competent dicastery of the Apostolic See (and not, e.g., to the metropolitan bishop or the apostolic nuncio). In religious institutes, recourse is first to be made to the competent superior within the institute as mentioned in the constitutions (e.g., the supreme moderator) and only afterward to the Apostolic See.

[14] If the recourse is to be made to the Apostolic See, it can either be sent directly to the competent dicastery or, alternatively, to the apostolic nunciature of one's own country, which will forward it to the Apostolic See.

of an advocate or procurator. Therefore, cc. 1481–1490 on advocates and procurators in judicial processes may be applied analogously.

The hierarchical superior decides the recourse with a decree. They have a wide range of possibilities. They can confirm the decree, declare it invalid, rescind or revoke it, or replace or modify it (see c. 1739). To confirm the decree means that the decision in the decree is upheld. To declare the decree invalid means that the decree is null due to some violation of law (e.g., procedural error). To rescind or revoke the decree means that the decree is withdrawn in its entirety. To replace the decree means that the superior revokes the original decree and regulates the matter differently with their own decree. To modify the decree means that the superior leaves the original decree in force but alters it in certain aspects.

If the recourse was decided by an authority below the Apostolic See (e.g., the supreme moderator of a religious institute), an administrative recourse against the decision is given to the competent hierarchical superior. The Apostolic See is the final instance. An appeal against the decision of the dicastery of the Apostolic See can be brought before the Apostolic Signatura.

Further reading: Justin E. A. Glyn, "The Right to Administrative Justice in Religious Institutes," *StudCan* 52 (2018): 103–38; Elizabeth MacDonough, "The Protection of Rights in Religious Institutes," *Jur* 46 (1986): 164–204.

Appeal to the Apostolic Signatura

According to the 1983 Code of Canon Law and *Praedicate Evangelium* 196–198, the Supreme Tribunal of the Apostolic Signatura has three areas of competence:

- supreme tribunal of ordinary jurisdiction (see c. 1445 §1; PE 196)

- administrative tribunal for the Roman Curia (see c. 1445 §2; PE 197)
- administrative institution of justice in disciplinary matters (see c. 1445 §3; PE 198)

The Apostolic Signatura is governed by its proper law (see PE 199). The *Lex propria of the Supreme Tribunal of the Apostolic Signatura* (hereafter, LPSA) currently in force was promulgated with the motu proprio *Antiqua Ordinatione* of June 21, 2008, by Pope Benedict XVI.[15] Some minor changes were made with the motu proprio *Munus Tribunalis* of February 28, 2024, by Pope Francis.[16]

Regarding contentious-administrative cases, the "Apostolic Signatura, as the administrative tribunal for the Roman Curia, adjudicates recourses against individual administrative acts, whether issued by the Dicasteries or the Secretariat of State or else approved by them, whenever it is contended that the act being impugned violated some law, either in the decision-making process or in the procedure employed" (PE 197 §1). Object of an appeal to the Apostolic Signatura, just as in the case of an administrative recourse, is an individual administrative act. In contrast to an administrative recourse, an action before the Apostolic Signatura is only admissible if a violation of the law in the substance of the decision (*in decernendo*) or in the procedure used (*in procedendo*) is asserted. Thus, an administrative act can be challenged before the Apostolic Signatura only because it is deemed illegitimate and not because

[15] English translation: *Jur* 75 (2015): 619–57, and https://www.vatican.va/roman_curia/tribunals/apost_signat/documents/trib_segnatura-apost_lex-propria-2024_en.html.

[16] There is currently no official English translation. The original Italian text is published in *OR* 164/52 (February 3, 2024): 11, and https://www.vatican.va/content/francesco/it/motu_proprio/documents/20240228-motu-proprio-munus-tribunalis.html.

it is deemed inopportune.[17] It is not possible to appeal against certain types of individual administrative acts before the Apostolic Signatura, namely those relating to *delicta graviora*, those regarding certain disciplinary measures of the Dicastery for the Doctrine of the Faith, and those approved by the pope *in forma specifica*.[18]

An appeal must be filed within the peremptory time limit of sixty useful days after the notification of the decree in question (see LPSA art. 34 §1).[19]

The Apostolic Signatura consists of cardinals and bishops as judges who are appointed by the pope (see art. 1 §1). The prefect is one of the cardinals chosen by the pope. In addition, priests can be appointed as members (see art. 1 §2). Sentencing is collegial. It is usually carried out by a college of five judges (see art. 21). The prefect is assisted by a secretary who directs the affairs and persons of the Apostolic Signatura (see art. 2 §1). Furthermore, the supreme tribunal consists of the promoter of justice, at least two substitute promoters of justice, the defender of the bond, the head of the chancery, and a suitable number of officials (art. 3). The prefect, the secretary, the promoter of justice and their substitutes, and the defender of the bond form the *Congressus*. In contentious-administrative cases, the promoter of justice acts impartially in favor of justice and truth (see art. 7 §2). The head of the chancery directs the

[17] See *Decretum Congressus* of May 13, 1997, Prot. N. 27013/96 CA, in William L. Daniel, ed., *Ministerium Iustitiae: Jurisprudence of the Supreme Tribunal of the Apostolic Signatura* (Wilson & Lafleur, 2011), 275–87: "*Ceterum, non pertinet ad hoc Supremum Tribunal videre utrum, necne, concreta decisio opportuna et prudens fuerit*" (286).

[18] It is problematic for the juridical protection of the persons concerned if a dicastery of the Apostolic See requests the pope's approval of a decree *in forma specifica* in order to terminate a procedure in progress before the Apostolic Signatura.

[19] All parenthetical references to articles ("art.") through the remainder of this section refer to articles of the LPSA.

chancery under the authority of the secretary (see art. 11 §1). Parties can stand in trial only through a procurator-advocate (see art. 16 §1). Advocates of the Roman Curia can assume the legal representation (see art. 17 §1). Advocates of the Roman Rota or other persons with a doctorate in canon law can be admitted *ad casum* by the prefect as procurator-advocate, provided they are truly experts in the material (see art. 17 §3).

The procedure for contentious-administrative cases is laid down in art. 73–104. It is initiated by a *libellus* of the recurrent (submitted by their advocate). The Apostolic Signatura charges fees. The norms regarding fees are to be established by the *Congressus* (see art. 30 §1). Upon receipt of the *libellus*, the recurrent needs to pay a deposit of (currently) €1,550. If a religious appeals, this amount must be paid by the institute. In addition, the parties will have to pay their own advocates. The institute must also pay the advocate of the religious if a religious lodges an appeal.[20] Having received the *libellus*, the secretary conducts some preliminary investigations to ascertain that the petition contains all the necessary formalities and that it does not manifestly lack any foundation. After having heard the promoter of justice, the secretary can reject a recourse by decree at the outset, if it manifestly lacks a presupposition or any foundation (see art. 76). Otherwise, the secretary accepts the recourse by decree. If the recourse is accepted, the secretary informs the competent dicastery of the Apostolic See and all other parties involved[21] and requests the relevant files (see art. 79). The promoter of justice submits their *votum pro rei veritate*, and written arguments are ex-

[20] The Apostolic Signatura charges a religious institute a total of €2,550, of which €1,550 is the fee of the Signatura and €1,000 is the fee of the advocate. The amount can be paid in euros directly to the Signatura or in local currency to the apostolic nunciature.

[21] E.g., the diocesan bishop or the religious superior, if the appeal has its roots in their decisions.

changed between the advocates of the parties (see art. 81–82). Further proof can be collected. Suspension of the execution of the challenged decree can be requested (see art. 95–100). According to the jurisprudence of the Apostolic Signatura, two criteria are decisive for granting a suspension of the execution: first, the likelihood of a positive decision and, second, the need for legal protection, that is, the difficulty of undoing the legal effects of the challenged decree in the case of a positive decision.[22] Next, the *Congressus* is convoked, and the prefect decides whether the recourse is to be admitted to discussion or rejected because it manifestly lacks a presupposition or any foundation (see art. 83 §1). If a recourse is admitted, the secretary convokes the promoter of justice and the advocates of the parties for an oral summary debate where the formula of the doubts is agreed upon (see art. 85 §1). Furthermore, a petition for the reparation of damages inflicted by an unlawful decree can be proposed (see art. 101). Afterward, the promoter of justice submits his *votum pro rei veritate*, and the advocates present their conclusive briefs. The statements are exchanged between the promoter of justice and the advocates. The advocates can present their responses, and the promoter of justice has the right to intervene last (see art. 88). Lastly, the college of judges meets and issues its decision (see art. 89; 46–49).

[22] See *Decretum Congressus* of November 13, 2015, Prot. N. 50461/15 CA in *IE* 29 (2017) 668–70: "*Pro comperto habito quod, iuxta communem H. S. T. iurisprudentiam, exsecutionis suspensio ex duobus elementis inter se conexis pendet: priore loco, ponderanda est probabilitas decisionis favorabilis relate ad recursum quo actus legitimitas impugnatur, adeo ut quanto maior est illa probabilitas, tanto plus suspensionis concessio urget, et versa vice; altero loco, diiudicanda est damnorum irreparabilitas in casu decisionis favorabilis, ita ut quanto plus actus administrativi impugnati exsecutio effectus parit, qui difficulter retrotrahi poterunt, tanto plus suspensionis concessio urget, et versa vice*" (668–69).

Further reading: Francesco D'Ostilio, "Gli istituti della vita consacrata nelle decisioni del Supremo Tribunale della Signatura Apostolica," *Claretianum* 27 (1987): 279–344; Kenneth K. Schwanger, "Contentious-Administrative Recourse before the Supreme Tribunal of the Apostolic Signatura," *Jur* 58 (1998): 171–97.

Bibliography

Acin, Mayong Andreas. "The Exclaustration of Religious. Law and Praxis." *StudCan* 56 (2022): 299–321.

Akpoghiran, Peter O. *The Catholic Formulary in Accordance with the Code of Canon Law*. Vol. 6a, *Canonical Institutes and Societies Acts*. CreateSpace, 2020.

Akpoghiran, Peter O. *The Catholic Formulary in Accordance with the Code of Canon Law*. Vol. 7a, *Eremitical and Order of Virgins Acts*. CreateSpace, 2020.

Álvarez Alonso, Fermina. "Consecration and Secular Life in the Second Vatican Council: The Contribution of the Secular Institutes." *Jur* 76 (2016): 43–67.

Austin, Brian T. "Canon 603: Transfer of a Diocesan Hermit or Hermitess." *RRAO* 2020: 114–17.

Austin, Rodger. "Commentary: Motu Proprio of Pope Francis Authenticum Charismatis." *The Canonist* 11 (2020): 189–96.

Awiti, Marren Rose A. "Formation during the Period of Temporary Vows According to the 1983 Code and the Subsequent Apostolic See Documents." *StudCan* 51 (1997): 391–439.

Bahíllo Ruiz, Teodoro. "Presencia de religiosos laicos en institutos clericales: institutos mixtos, ¿posibilidad real o vía sin salida?" *Estudios eclesiásticos* 89 (2014): 675–99.

Bahíllo Ruiz, Teodoro. *Los religiosos ausentes de la casa religiosa según el canon 665*. Ediurcla, 1994.

Bamberg, Anne. "Monasterio autónomo y vigilancia particular del Obispo diocesano: En torno a la interpretación del c. 615 del Código de Derecho Canónico." *IC* 48 (2008): 477–92.

Bauer, Nancy. "'Ecclesiae sponsae imago': Instruction on the Order of Consecrated Virgins: Aids in Implementing Canon 604 and the Rite of Consecration." *Jur* 77 (2021): 73–101.

Bauer, Nancy. "The Lengthening Duration of Initial Formation in Religious Institutes: Historical-Canonical Overview." *StudCan* 55 (2021): 147–67.

Bauer, Nancy. "Moniales et sorores: The Canonical Distinction Between Nuns and Sisters with Particular Reference to Benedictine Women Religious." *ABR* 70 (2019): 45–73.

Bauer, Nancy. "The Religious Habit in Church Law from 1917 to the Present." *StudCan* 52 (2018): 45–80.

Bauer, Nancy. "Three Perspectives on Obedience: Benedict of Nursia, Ignatius of Loyola and the 1983 Code of Canon Law." *Jur* 65 (2005): 55–97.

Beal, John P. "Charism, Mission, and Canon Law: Management as Ministry." *StudCan* 55 (2021): 169–94.

Beal, John P., James A. Coriden, and Thomas J. Green, eds. *New Commentary on the Code of Canon Law*. Paulist, 2000.

Beyer, Jean. *Il diritto della vita consacrata*. Ancora, 1989.

Beyer, Jean. *A New Way of Apostolic Consecrated Life: The Secular Institute*. Pontificia Università Gregoriana, 1967.

Beyer, Jean. "Prospects for the Reform of Religious Constitutions." *The Way Supplement* 26 (1975): 84–96.

Canadian Conference of Catholic Bishops. *Program for Priestly Formation (Ratio formationis sacerdotalis nationalis) for English-speaking Canada*. CCCB, 2022.

Casey, Maria. "The Evolution of New Forms of Consecrated Life." *StudCan* 36 (2002): 463–86.

Cerletty, Miriam. "Some Practical Helps for the Development of Constitutions." *Studia canonica* 14 (1980): 155–70.

Cheruvilparambil, Rosmin. "Transfer between Religious Institutions: Requirements, Process and Effects." *Iustitia: Dharmaram Journal of Canon Law* 11 (2020): 187–201.

Ciardi, Fabio. "Il carisma del fondatore." *Annales theologici* 30 (2016): 141–58.

Code of Canon Law: Latin-English Edition. 4th printing. Canon Law Society of America, 2023.

Code of Canons of the Eastern Churches. Latin-English Edition. Canon Law Society of America, 2001.

Cogan, Patrick. "Exclaustration and Social Security and Pension Benefits." *RRAO* 2006: 56–57.

Cogan, Patrick J., ed. *Selected Issues in Religious Law*. Canon Law Society of America, 1997.

Congregatio pro doctrina fidei. "Professio fidei et iusiurandum fidelitatis in suscipiendo officio nomine Ecclesiae exercendo una cum nota doctrinali adnexa" (29 iunii 1998). *AAS* 90 (1998): 542–51.

Congregation for Institutes of Consecrated Life and Societies of Apostolic Life. "Circular Letter on the Motu Proprio of Pope Francis *Communis Vita*." *RRAO* 2020: 24–27.

Congregation for Institutes of Consecrated Life and Societies of Apostolic Life. "Circular Letter to General Moderators." Prot. N. Sp.R. 2452/20. *RRAO* 2020: 13–15.

Congregation for Institutes of Consecrated Life and Societies of Apostolic Life. *Cor Orans: Instruction on the Implementation of the Apostolic Constitution Vultum Dei quaerere on Women's Contemplative Life*. Libreria Editrice Vaticana, 2018.

Congregation for Institutes of Consecrated Life and Societies of Apostolic Life. *Ecclesiae Sponsae Imago: Instruction on the Ordo Virginum*. Libreria Editrice Vaticana, 2021.

Congregation for Institutes of Consecrated Life and Societies of Apostolic Life. *Economy at the Service of Charism and Mission*. Libreria Editrice Vaticana, 2018.

Congregation for Institutes of Consecrated Life and Societies of Apostolic Life. *Fraternal Life in Community (Congregavit Nos in Unum Christi Amor)*. Pauline, 1994.

Congregation for Institutes of Consecrated Life and Societies of Apostolic Life. *The Gift of Fidelity, The Joy of Perseverance*. Libreria Editrice Vaticana, 2020.

Congregation for Institutes of Consecrated Life and Societies of Apostolic Life. *Guidelines for the Administration of the Assets in Institutes of Consecrated Life and in Societies of Apostolic Life*. Libreria Editrice Vaticana, 2014.

Congregation for Institutes of Consecrated Life and Societies of Apostolic Life. *The Hermit's Way of Life in the Local Church*. Libreria Editrice Vaticana, 2022.

Congregation for Institutes of Consecrated Life and Societies of Apostolic Life. *Identity and Mission of the Religious Brother in the Church*. Libreria Editrice Vaticana, 2015.

Congregation for Institutes of Consecrated Life and Societies of Apostolic Life. *On Inter-Institute Collaboration for Formation*. www.vatican.va/roman_curia/congregations/ccscrlife/documents/rc_con_ccscrlife_doc_08121998_inter-formation_en.html.

Congregation for Institutes of Consecrated Life and Societies of Apostolic Life. *Potissimum Institutioni: On Formation in Religious Institutes*. www.vatican.va/roman_curia/congregations/ccscrlife/documents/rc_con_ccscrlife_doc_02021990_directives-on-formation_en.html.

Congregation for Institutes of Consecrated Life and Societies of Apostolic Life. *The Service of Authority and Obedience (Faciem Tuam, Domine, Requiram): Instruction*. Pauline, 2008.

Congregation for Institutes of Consecrated Life and Societies of Apostolic Life. "Suggested Guidelines for the Preparation of Periodic Reports on the Status and Life of Institutes of Consecrated Life and Societies of Apostolic Life." Prot. N. SpR 640/2008. *Studies in Church Law* 5 (2009): 41–44.

Congregation for Religious and Secular Institutes. "Participation by Lay Religious in Government of Clerical Institutes." *CLD* 7: 468–69.

Congregation for Religious and Secular Institutes and Congregation for Bishops. *Mutuae Relationes*. USCCB, 2004.

Congregation for the Doctrine of the Faith. *Instruction on Some Aspects of the Use of the Instruments of Social Communication in Promoting the Doctrine of the Faith*. Pauline, 1992.

Conn, James J. "Bishops and the Apostolates of Religious." *CLSA Proceedings* 57 (1995): 49–83.

Costa, Maurizi. "Il governo del superiore e il suo consiglio: Dati canonici e rilettura spirituale." *PRC* 93 (2001). 189–221.

Daniel, William L., ed. *Ministerium Iustitiae: Jurisprudence of the Supreme Tribunal of the Apostolic Signatura*. Wilson & Lafleur, 2011.

Daniel, William L., ed. *Ministerium Iustitiae*. Vol. II, *The "Lex propria" and More Recent Contentious-Administrative Jurisprudence of the Supreme Tribunal of the Apostolic Signatura*. Wilson & Lafleur, 2021.

Darcy, Catherine. "Right to Withhold or Obligation to Disclose Reasons for Dismissal of a Novice or Extending the Novitiate." *RRAO* 1995: 52–55.

De Boccard, Nicolas. *Charisme et instituts de vie consacré: Les canons 578 et 587 du code de droit canonique de 1983*. Romanité et modernité du droit 22. DeBoccard, 2015.

Dicastery for Institutes of Consecrated Life and Societies of Apostolic Life. "Circular Letter on the Utilization of Computer-Telematic Tools for Acts of Governance Referred to in Canons 627, 127 and 166." Prot. N. Sp.R. 2452/20. *RRAO* 2023: 46–47.

Doskey, Clinton J. "Declaration of Nullity: Its Effect on Admission to Clerical and Religious Life." *CLSA Proceedings* 47 (1985): 115–23.

D'Ostilio, Francesco. "Gli istituti della vita consacrata nelle decisioni del Supremo Tribunale della Signatura Apostolica." *Claretianum* 27 (1987): 279–344.

D'Souza, Victor G. "Admission of Married Catholics into Religious Institutes." *Studies in Church Law* 6 (2010): 403–13.

D'Souza, Victor G. "Automatic Dismissal of the Religious from the Religious Institute on the Ground of Marriage." *Studies in Church Law* 6 (2010): 445–52.

D'Souza, Victor G. "Religious Habit and Ecclesiastical Dress: Canon Law and Ecclesial Values." *Indian Theological Studies* 40 (2003): 323–56.

Ekot, Maria-Stella Joseph. *Administration of Temporal Goods of Religious Institutes According to the Teachings of the Church and the Codes of Canon Law*. Pontificia Università Gregoriana, 2022.

Emsley, Nichola. "The Rite of Consecration of Virgins." In *Handbook for Liturgical Studies*. Vol. IV, *Sacraments and Sacramentals*. Edited by Anscar J. Chupungco. Liturgical Press, 2000.

Esposito, Bruno. “La partecipazione del superiore religioso alle votazioni con il suo consiglio quando il diritto richiede il consenso: Questione risolta? Alcune riflessioni sui cann. 127 § 1 e 627.” *PRC* 95 (2006): 37–68.

Etzi, Priamo. “Il consiglio del superiore religioso: Normativa e dibattiti (cann. 627 e 127).” VC 39 (2003): 612–35.

Euart, Sharon A. “Religious Institutes and the Juridical Relationship of the Members to the Institute.” *Jur* 51 (1991): 103–18.

Finn, Thomas J. “An Old Entity—A New Name: Societies of Apostolic Life.” *StudCan* 20 (1986): 439–56.

Francis. *The Apostolic Constitution “Preach the Gospel” (*Praedicate Evangelium*): With an Appraisal of Francis’s Reform of the Roman Curia by Massimo Faggioli.* Liturgical Press, 2022.

Francis. “Apostolic Letter *Authenticum charismatis.*” *RRAO* 2021: 59–60.

Francis. “Apostolic Letter *Communis vita.*” *RRAO* 2019: 25–26.

Francis. “Apostolic Letter *Competentias quasdam.*” *RROA* 2022: 50–55.

Francis. “Apostolic Letter *Expedit ut iura.*” *RROA* 2023: 58–59.

Francis. “Apostolic Letter *Recognitum Librum VI.*” *RRAO* 2022: 56.

Francis. “Rescript ex Audientia Concerning Canon 579 of the Code of Canon Law on the Erection of a Diocesan Institute.” *RRAO* 2016: 10–11.

Francis. “Rescriptum ex Audientia Ss.Mi. Rescript of the Holy Father Francis Regarding the Derogation from Can. 588 § 2 CIC.” *RRAO* 2022: 57.

Futrell, John C. “Discovering the Founder’s Charism.” *The Way* 14 (1971): 62–70.

Galante, Joseph A. “Consecrated Life: New Forms and New Institutes.” *CLSA Proceedings* 48 (1986): 118–25.

Galante, Joseph A. “The Relationship of the Diocesan Bishop and Institutes of Pontifical Right.” *CLSA Proceedings* 57 (1995): 90–96.

Gallen, Joseph F. “Guide for Conforming Constitutions to the New Code.” *RfR* 42 (1983): 748–58.

Gallen, Joseph F. "Writing Constitutions." *RfR* 36 (1977): 773–87.

García Martín, Julio. "La potestad de los superiores religiosos de los institutos religiosos laicales de derecho pontificio." *CpRM* 85 (2004): 31–75.

Geisinger, Robert. "Some Ongoing Considerations in Canon Law for Treasurers General of Religious Institutes." *PRC* 95 (2006): 227–59.

Gerhartz, Johannes Günter. *"Insuper promitto . . .": Die feierlichen Sondergelübde katholischer Orden*. Series Facultatis Iuris Canonici / B 19. Editrice Pontificia Università Gregoriana, 1966.

Giovanelli, Giorgio. "The Investigatio Praevia and the Role of the Ordinary for Criminal Procedures." *The Canonist* 13 (2022): 217–27.

Glyn, Justin E. A. "The Right to Administrative Justice in Religious Institutes." *StudCan* 52 (2018): 103–38.

Gomes, Evaldo X. "Readmissão de candidatos à vida religiosa segundo o cânone 690 do Código de Direito Canônico." *Direito e pastoral* 17 (2003): 45–53.

Gonzales, Javier. "Basic Procedures Pertinent to Religious Institutes: Transfer, Exclaustration, Departure and Dismissal." *Philippine Canonical Forum* 5 (2003): 147–90.

Gonzales, Javier. "From Diocesan to Pontifical Right: The Shifting of a Religious Institute." *Philippine Canonical Forum* 11 (2009): 259–69.

Gottemoeller, Doris. "Religious Habits Reconsidered." *RfR* 68 (2009): 181–91.

Graham, Joanne. "The Relation between Religious Institutes and the Diocese." *CLSA Proceedings* 60 (1998): 82–90.

Henseler, Rudolf. "Vom institutum iuris diocesani zum institutum iuris pontificii: Die zwölf Erfordernisse." In *Veritas vos liberabit*, edited by Matthias Pulte. Schöningh, 2017.

Hereford, Amy. "Canon 644: Education Loans of Those Entering Religious Communities." *RRAO* 2010: 114–15.

Hereford, Amy. *See I Am Making Something New: New Institutes, Diocesan Hermits and Consecrated Virgins and New Forms of Consecrated Life*. CreateSpace, 2018.

Hernández Rodríguez, María V. "I fedeli associati agli istituti secolari: Genesi e fonti del can. 725." *ME* 126 (2001): 437–57.

Herranz Casado, Julián. "The Evolution of Secular Institutes." *Jur* 25 (1965): 129–62.

Hill, Richard A. "An Overview of *Mutuae Relationes*." In *Code, Community, Ministry: Selected Studies for the Parish Minister Introducing the Revised Code of Canon Law*, edited by James H. Provost Canon Law Society of America, 1983.

Hip-Flores, Christina. "Consecrated Widows: Altars of God: A Restored Ancient Vocation in the Catholic Church." *Logos: A Journal of Catholic Thought and Culture* 22 (2019): 108–30.

Holland, Sharon. "Bishop and Religious: Right Relationship for Ecclesial Mission." *CLSA Proceedings* 73 (2011): 108–17.

Holland, Sharon. "Religious House According to Canon 608." *Jur* 50 (1990): 524–52.

Huels, John M. "The Demise of Religious Exemption." *Jur* 54 (1994): 40–55.

Jaramillo, Eileen C. "Canon 644: Addressing Debts before Entering a Religious Institute." *RRAO* 2010: 110–13.

Jaramillo, Eileen C. "Erection as an Institute of Consecrated Life or a Society of Apostolic Life: The Nuts and Bolts." *CLSA Proceedings* 80 (2018): 153–73.

John Paul II. *The Consecrated Life: Vita Consecrata: Post-Synodal Apostolic Exhortation*. United States Catholic Conference, 1996.

Kaptijn, Astrid. "Submission of the Will and Violation of the Vow of Obedience: Contributions to the Discussion of Canon 601." *Jur* 56 (1996): 307–37.

Kay, David J. *Exemption: Origins of Exemption and Vatican Council II*. Editrice Pontificia Università Gregoriana, 1990.

Knowles, David. *Christian Monasticism*. Weidenfeld & Nicolson, 1969.

Knowles, David. *From Pachomius to Ignatius: A Study in the Constitutional History of the Religious Orders*. Clarendon, 1966.

Koluthara, Varghese. "Religious and the Administration of Temporal Goods." *Iustitia: Dharmaram Journal of Canon Law* 9 (2018): 95–108.

Koonamparampil, Joseph. "Clerical Obligations Applied to the Religious: An Exegesis of Can. 672." *CpRM* 69 (1988): 111–44 (part 1/3), 271–84 (part 2/3), 365–83 (part 3/3).

Kozlowski, John Chrysostom. "When an Illegitimate Absence Irreparably Damages Communion: An Analysis of the Motu Proprio *Communis Vita*." *Angelicum* 99 (2022): 231–51.

MacDonald, Helen. "Hermits: The Juridical Implications of Canon 603." *StudCan* 26 (1992): 163–90.

MacDonough, Elizabeth. "The Protection of Rights in Religious Institutes." *Jur* 46 (1986): 164–204.

Mahoney, Kathleen A., ed. *Handbook on Educational Debt and Vocations to Religious Life*. National Religious Vocation Conference, 2013. www.nrvc.net/download/1532/educational_debt_handbook_3-2-14.pdf.

Malone, Anthony. "Commentary on Pope Francis' Motu Proprio *Communis Vita*." *The Canonist* 10 (2019): 12–15.

Marini, Francis J. "Readmission of Former Member of Religious Institute." *RRAO* 2006: 174–76.

McDermott, Rose. "Admission to the Noviciate with Declaration of Nullity." *RRAO* 1998: 58–59.

McDermott, Rose. "Associates and Associations Joined to Religious Institutes." *CLSA Proceedings* 60 (1998): 132–49.

McDermott, Rose. "Canon 636: Finance Officer in a Religious Institute." *RRAO* 2020: 118–19.

McDermott, Rose. "Canon 702, § 2: Equity and Charity to Separated Members," *CLSA Proceedings* 52 (1990): 120–33.

McDermott, Rose. "Ecclesiastical Authority and Religious Autonomy: Canon 679 under Glass." *StudCan* 38 (2004): 461–80.

McDermott, Rose. "The Financial Administrator of a Religious Institute." *RRAO* 1997: 58–59.

McDermott, Rose. "Fostering Communion between the Apostolic See and Religious Institutes and Societies of Apostolic Life: 2008 Guidelines for the Report in Canon 592 § 1." *Jur* 72 (2012): 428–52.

McDermott, Rose. "Governance in Religious Institutes: Structures of Participation and Representation. Canons 631–633." *Jur* 69 (2009): 442–71.

McDermott, Rose. "The Role of Councils in Religious Institutes." *Studies in Church Law* 5 (2009): 201–24.

McDermott, Rose. "The Service of Authority and Obedience: The Canonical Visitation of Major Superiors (Canon 628 §§ 1,3)." *StudCan* 99 (2010): 527–55.

McDermott, Rose. "Stewards of Gifts to Be Shared: The Vow of Poverty in Religious Life." *Studies in Church Law* 3 (2007): 95–128.

McDermott, Rose. "The Vigilance of the Diocesan or Eparchial Bishop: Diocesan / Eparchial Right Institutes / Sui iuris Monasteries / Hermits / Ascetics / Virgins / Widows." *Studies in Church Law* 8 (2012): 141–74.

Michl, Andrea. "'In saeculo et ex saeculo': Characteristics of the Secular Institutes." *Warszawskie Studia Teologiczne* 34 (2021): 196–211.

Michowicz, Przemysław. "Legal Difficulties and/or Impossibility Concerning New Forms of Consecrated Life (c. 605)." *StudCan* 48 (2014): 171–88.

Miller, Donna, and Eileen C. Jaramillo, eds. *Procedural Handbook for Institutes of Consecrated Life and Societies of Apostolic Life*. Canon Law Society of America, 2021.

Morrisey, Francis G. "The Directory for the Administration of Temporal Goods in Religious Institutes." In *Unico Ecclesiae Servitio: Canonical Studies Presented to Germain Lesage, O.M.I., on the Occasion of His 75th Birthday and of the 50th Anniversary of His Presbyterial Ordination*, edited by Michel Thériault. Faculty of Canon Law, Saint Paul University, 1991.

Morrisey, Francis G. "New Directives from the Holy See on the Administration of Temporal Goods for Institutes of Consecrated Life and Societies of Apostolic Life." *Studies in Church Law* 14 (2019): 227–58.

Noguchi, Takayoshi. "La naturaleza clerical, laical y 'mixta' de los institutos religiosos del CIC 83." *Cuadernos doctorales* 20 (2003): 195–235.

O'Malley, John W. "The Fourth Vow in Its Ignatian Context: A Historical Study." *Studies in the Spirituality of Jesuits* 15 (1983): 1–59.

Opondo, Jacinta Auma. *Temporary Profession and Exclusion from Subsequent Profession (cann. 655; 689): Theological-juridical Study*. Tesi gregoriana / Serie diritto canonico 106. Editrice Pontificia Università Gregoriana, 2017.

Paul VI. "Litterae Apostolicae *Ministeria quaedam*." *AAS* 64 (1972): 529–34.

Perlasca, Alberto. "L'interpretazione autentica delle leggi ecclesiali: Il superiore e il suo consiglio (can. 127 § 1)." *QDE* 23 (2010): 311–23.

Perlasca, Alberto. "Rescriptum ex audientia SS.mi circa l'erezione degli istituti diocesani di vita consacrata (can. 579)." *QDE* 30 (2017): 351–57.

Pinheiro, Antony. "Bishops-Religious Relationship (can. 678, §§ 1–2)." *CpRM* 68 (1987): 35–76.

Pius IX. "Litterae encyclicae *Neminem latet*." In *Collectanea in usum secretariae Sacrae Congregationis Episcoporum et Regularium*, edited by Giuseppe Andrea Bizzarri. Tipografia poliglotta, 1885.

Pombo Oncins, Diego Eugenio. "La responsabilità dei Superiori nell'ammissione all'Istituto (cann. 597, 641-645)." *PRC* 107 (2015): 591–610.

Provost, James H. "Clergy and Religious in Political Office: Canonical Comments in the American Context." *Jur* 44 (1984): 276–303.

Provost, James H. "Manner of Superior Seeking Council's Consent." *RRAO* 1995: 38–39.

Purcell, Thomas F. *The Training of Members of Religious Institutes for Ordained Ministry According to the Current Law of the Church*. Canon Law Studies 537. Catholic University of America Press, 2001.

Rava, Alfredo. "Il governo degli istituti di vita consacrata in tempo di Covid-19." *QDE* 36 (2023): 448–63.

Recchi, Silvia. "Strutture di partecipazione negli Istituti di vita consacrata." *QDE* 1 (1988): 52–59.

Renken, John A. "Acts of Extraordinary Administration of Ecclesiastical Goods in Book V of the CIC." *StudCan* 49 (2015): 577–96.

Renken, John A. "The Stable Patrimony of Public Juridic Persons." *Jur* 70 (2010): 131–62.

Reyes, Melanie S. "A Comparative Study of Sacred Bonds in Institutes of Consecrated Life." *Philippiniana Sacra* 54 (2019): 219–40.

Rocca, Giancarlo. "Il Carisma del Fondatore." *Claretianum* 34 (1994): 31–105.

Romano, Francesco. "I superiori del canone 596 nel corpo sociale della Chiesa." *Teresianum* 57 (2006): 391–448.

Sánchez-Girón Renedo, José Luis. "Sentido y finalidad de un privilegio relativo al c. 630." *Estudios Eclesiásticos* 81 (2006): 725–60.

Schumacher, William A., and J. James Cuneo. "Exclaustration." *RRAO* 1985: 20–23.

Schwanger, Kenneth K. "Contentious-Administrative Recourse before the Supreme Tribunal of the Apostolic Signatura." *Jur* 58 (1998): 171–97.

Sebastian, Arul Kumar. *Religious Elevated to Episcopate: A Historical, Theological and Juridical Approach in CIC/1983*. Pontificia Università Gregoriana, 2022.

Second Vatican Council. *Christus Dominus: Decree on the Pastoral Office of Bishops in the Church*. In Austin Flannery, ed., *Vatican Council II: Constitutions, Decrees, Declarations: A Completely Revised Translation in Inclusive Language*. Liturgical Press, 2014.

Second Vatican Council. *Perfectae Caritatis: Decree on the Up-to-Date Renewal of Religious Life*. In Flannery, *Vatican Council II*.

Shea, Patrick T. "Exclaustration." *CLSA Proceedings* 59 (1997): 267–81.

Sheridan, Sean O. "Consecrated Virgins and Hermits." *Jur* 73 (2013): 493–512.

Sheridan, Sean O. "To Seek the Face of God: The Cloister and Renewal of Women's Contemplative Monasteries." *Jur* 76 (2016): 415–46.

Skorupa, Ambroży. "Participation of Religious Brothers in the Exercise of Authority in Clerical Religious Institutes." *KiP* 12 (2023): 201–14.

Smith, Rosemary. "The Personal Patrimony of Individual Members of Religious Institutes: Current Issues." *CLSA Proceedings* 62 (2000): 263–81

Sugawara, Yuji. "Amministrazione e alienazione dei beni temporali degli Istituti religiosi nel Codice (can. 638)." *PRC* 97 (2008): 251–82.

Sugawara, Yuji. "Concetto teologico e giuridico del 'carisma di fondazione' degli istituti di vita consacrata." *PRC* 91 (2002): 239–71.

Sugawara, Yuji. "La povertà evangelica nel codice: Norma comune (can. 600) e applicazione individuale (can. 668)." *PRC* 89 (2000): 45–77.

Sugawara, Yuji. *Religious Poverty: From Vatican Council II to the 1994 Synod of Bishops*. Tesi Gregoriana / Serie Diritto Canonico 3. Pontificia Università Gregoriana, 1997.

Sugawara, Yuji. "Ruolo delle Costituzioni negli Istituti di vita consacrata." *PRC* 98 (2009): 663–91.

Sullivan, Therese G. "Canons 125; 205; 219; 573-606; 641-661; 675: Suitability of Persons with Transsexualism." *RRAO* 2019: 39–44.

Thattil, Navya. "Distinctive Motives for Dismissal of Religious in CIC and CCEO." *Iustitia: Dharmaram Journal of Canon Law* 5 (2014): 205–24.

Tibi, Daniel. "L'adeguata armonizzazione degli elementi spirituali e giuridici nelle costituzioni (can. 587 § 3)." *QDE* 35 (2022): 82–90.

Tibi, Daniel. "'The Gift of Fidelity, the Joy of Perseverance.' Separation from Religious Institutes According to the Latest Roman Documents." *RfR* 3 (2023): 47–61.

Tiongco, Isaias Antonio. "La Naturaleza de la Potestad en los Institutos Religiosos a la luz de las Codificaciones de 1917 y de 1983." *Philippiniana Sacra* 46 (2011): 3–29.

United States Conference of Catholic Bishops. *Program of Priestly Formation in the United States of America*. 6th ed. United States Conference of Catholic Bishops, 2022.

Werner, Philipp. *Klostermanagement im Team: Praktische Fallstudie über die Einrichtung eines Wirtschaftsrates in einer Benediktinerabtei, seine rechtliche Gestaltung und praktische Arbeit*. Kanonistische Reihe 34. EOS, 2022.

Yetukuri, Showri Raju. "General Governance in the Societies of Apostolic Life." *Scientia Canonica* 3 (2020): 99–141.